THE BUSINESS OF LEGAL:

THE DATA-DRIVEN LAW PRACTICE

by

Mary Juetten

TP

TELEMACHUS PRESS

THE BUSINESS OF LEGAL: THE DATA-DRIVEN LAW PRACTICE

Post-it® is a registered trademark of 3M

Cover designed by Telemachus Press, LLC

Cover art:
Copyright © iStockPhoto/640004460_-slav-
Copyright © iStockPhoto/958260376_PhonlamaiPhoto

Published by Telemachus Press, LLC
7652 Sawmill Road
Suite 304
Dublin, Ohio 43016
http://www.telemachuspress.com

Visit the author website:
http://www.maryjuetten.com

LAW/Law Office Management
BUSINESS & ECONOMICS/Management

ISBN: 978-1-948046-21-3 (eBook)
ISBN: 978-1-948046-22-0 (Paperback)

Library of Congress Location Number: 2018955765

Version 2018.09.10

Acknowledgements

For this book, I chatted with the amazing lawyers listed below to help create the fictitious firms for this book and gather time management and technology tips.

Ruth Carter, Venjuris Innovation Counsel

Patrick Palace & Jordan Couch, Palace Law

Juliet Peters, Framework Legal, PLLC

Maria Crimi Speth, Jaburg | Wilk

Mindy Yocum, Yocum Law Office

A huge thank you to these six attorneys plus the usual suspects in my legal tech life and the countless other lawyers I run into on social media or in real life. And, of course, I rely on my non-legal colleagues who run businesses or are other professionals, all with best practices that inspired me to pull this together.

A final huge extra thank you to Jordan Couch for his feedback as the first reader besides my extremely patient husband-editor.

To my team gluten: Philip, Ashley, and Jake are always there for me and who have taught me to own my crazy ways.

Table of Contents

Introduction

One of my favorite law school classes was Legal Drafting, which focused on using plain English and avoiding jargon. Like that class, this book is jargon-free. All trendy words have been excluded. I will simply explain how you and your team can improve the firm's bottom line and ensure your clients are happy using data and information that you already have.

I recently cleaned out my closet for a move and parted with some really cool clothes from my pre-kid years. My daughter, who just graduated college, was thrilled to receive them, and she immediately decided they were "vintage." Like my clothes, many business management strategies are also vintage. They keep coming back, renamed with new buzz words. We will use these vintage, tried and true management techniques to help solve your firm's problems, but we will skip the buzz words.

Who is This Book For?

Any lawyer, anywhere, but especially small-firm managers and owners. I have spoken and worked with attorneys around the world and while the laws may differ, the core of the business and management is universal.

In addition, this book is not just for tech-savvy lawyers. In fact, you should learn the concepts in this book *before* you try to solve your problems with technology.

How to Use This Book

I created two fictitious firms to illustrate the concepts in this book. The first firm, Ferndale Family Law LLP (FFL), has two partners and three associates, plus a paralegal and legal assistant. FFL has operated for about six years and faces many of the challenges that similar-sized firms deal with:

- FFL needs more clients and a more efficient intake process;

- Time management is a constant challenge for everyone at FFL;

- Associates are not sure of the firm's objectives or how to help the firm succeed;

- Usually there is a cash crunch at the end of the month; and

- Everyone at FFL feels the work is not getting done efficiently but doesn't necessarily know why.

These problems are common to most small law firms, but solos often face different challenges, especially when they start a new firm. One of FFL's associates will strike out on his own and serve as our second firm to study.

You can read this book from cover to cover or go straight to the chapters or appendices that reflect your current needs. You choose. Onwards!

THE BUSINESS OF LEGAL:
THE DATA-DRIVEN LAW PRACTICE

Your Firm's Raison d´être

Before we study each firm, let's zoom out and consider the big picture of why your firm exists. Does your firm exist because law is your calling, it is a means to pay your bills, it is a way to solve clients' problems, or for some other reason?

What problems are you and your firm trying to solve? What value does your firm create? Before you start trying to change things at your firm, take the time to establish the reason for your firm's existence in the first place.

What is a lawyer?

First, let's get existential and look briefly at how the trends shaping the future of law practice may impact your firm and the way you define your role as a lawyer. Webster's dictionary defines a *lawyer* as a person who represents clients in a court of law or advises or acts for them in other legal matters. The Oxford Thesaurus provides the following alternatives to the word lawyer: counsel, advocate, legal practitioner, member of the bar, attorney, and counselor at law. And of course, *solicitor* and *barrister* are the common terms in the UK.

I asked a number of lawyers across the country how they define themselves in 2017. Their one-word definitions included: advocate, problem-solver, counsel, advisor, connector, translator, legal-inventor, and mitigator. Most avoided using the words *legal* and *law* other than to say that part of their role is to translate the law or legalese in order to solve their clients' problems.

What do you wish to do?

We all attended law school and it was a grueling time. Like many before me, I read Scott Turow's *One L: The Turbulent True Story of a First Year at Harvard Law School* before my first year at Sandra Day O'Connor College of Law (Arizona State University) in Tempe, Arizona. In Turow's afterword, written a decade after graduation, he described the high anxiety and unhealthy competition during the "forced march" of the remaining two years of law school.

One of the things that struck me was this comment: "In spite of the prominence of law, lawyers themselves are far less regarded. Many lay people do not like lawyers. And to a surprising extent, lawyers often do not like themselves." Couple that with the struggle that is faced by most professions; how to do well while doing good. It seems we are forced to choose between helping others and earning a good living.

Most importantly, for most, our legal education is not "lawyer school" unless you had a meaningful clinic or internship. We attend law school to learn how to "think like a lawyer." But we do not learn how to handle a project or matter, let alone how to start and grow a law firm.

I have spoken to many lawyers who wish that they had taken a business or accounting class. However, much of what works well in business you either learned in grade school or as you started your adult life, not in university. This brings to mind the Golden Rule, which is my mantra both professionally and personally: "Do to others what you want them to do to you." In other words, have empathy for your team, clients, friends, and family and remember some fundamentals from your early years.

Below are some of my favorite instructions from Robert Fulghum's book, *All I Really Need to Know I Learned in Kindergarten*. I have taken the liberty of adjusting them to the legal setting:

1. **Share everything.** Obviously not confidential information but be open with your partners and team, and be receptive to suggestions and ideas.

2. **Play fair.** Building upon the "do unto others" idea, creating an open and honest work environment requires you to lead by example and be fair.

3. **Don't hit people.** Adjusted for your firm, this means do not surprise or blame people, particularly in group settings.

4. **Put things back where you found them.** More than returning items, it's important to make things right and ensure that you stay within your area of expertise.

5. **CLEAN UP YOUR OWN MESS.** I'm not referring to the lunch room, but that is important too. If you make a mistake, own it and fix it. Your team is not around to take the fall for your errors.

There are more from Fulghum listed in Appendix A, but keep the above in mind as you read this book.

In summary, lawyers spend too much time on non-lawyer work. As reported in Clio's legal trends report for 2016 and 2017, about 75% or 6 hours per day is spent on administration including marketing and billing. This book will help you make the necessary decisions based on data to free yourself up to practice law.

Is Your Firm Set Up for Success?

Many of the firms that I have spoken with do not have a defined business model or process, with or without administrative help. Further, many small firms do not set up teams for each matter with a lead because the partners wish to control all the work. The "might as well do it myself to get it right the first time" attitude seems to be widespread among law firms. Add in the competition for both billable hours and clients, and it's not a surprise that many firms suffer from a lack of systems and delegation, not to mention limited teamwork and a high level of unhealthy competition.

There is no training in law school on how to work together as a team like there is in the business, accounting, engineering and arts schools. I did almost no work in teams while attending law school. More commonly, law school pits one student against another (moot court and grading on the curve) further degrading the mindset that efficiency and value can be attained by working together with a common goal in mind.

Once out of law school, even a solo must work with clients, other lawyers, courts and agencies. You should also be outsourcing work like accounting and tax preparation, which means collaborating with independent contractors. However, lawyers sometimes let competitiveness take over, ruining partnerships because, in general, lawyers do not cooperate and instead revert to the competitive adversarial positions. At a recent event, when asked about managing potential clients using collaborative sales technology, an older lawyer said he would never share his potential client leads with any other attorney at his firm and would never put potential client information into a shared customer relationship management solution. This type of behavior leads to big problems for small firms.

Many lawyers are control freaks and find it difficult to delegate or outsource work. In comparison, most successful businesses involve collaborative teams. Successful professionals may even develop a work persona separate from their home personality in order to work better with their team.

Data-driven decision making requires and lends itself to transparency, delegation and collaboration in order to optimize the firm's performance. You will have to work with your team to identify pain points, bottlenecks, issues and underperforming areas, and to focus on working with the best clients for your firm.

Start with the End in Mind

What will success look like to you and your practice or firm? There is no right answer, but you should start with the end in mind. Whether it's a new hire, a change in process, or a new matter. What is the ultimate desired outcome? Apply the same thinking to your entire practice. The goal of this book is to help you get away from feeling like you are on a treadmill and working hard for disappointing results. By working towards your end goal using data, you can get out in front of your results and grow your firm.

Years ago, I worked for then PricewaterhouseCoopers as a Process Re-Engineering Consultant (PwC's term). Process re-engineering was around long before I gave birth to the same college-graduate who is now taking my vintage clothes. I won't use that buzzword again, but it's the same management technique we will be using as we walk through how to review your firm's day-to-day operations and the flow of clients and client work.

You do not need any special skills to use this book, just an inquisitive mind. Asking questions and reading carefully will serve you well, just like it has since kindergarten. At five, my son was on a remote island fishing trip and was dubbed Captain Question by the staff because he was constantly asking how everything worked and why. Some of the smartest people I know do the same thing, consistently and respect-fully. In fact, much of the work that I did in the 1990s for PwC con-sisted of asking *Why?* and *So What?* in order to challenge the status quo. The same approach has now been incorporated into "design thinking" but it's actually just a simple approach that we will walk through using examples, ignoring unnecessary terms like *process re-engineering* and *design thinking*.

Remember that running a business is like managing a large project that is made up of a series of small projects. In your life, you have probably planned a birthday party or maybe even a wedding. The same skill set for planning a party is all that is required for using this book successfully. Just break the work down into manageable chunks and get started.

Do not be afraid to go outside the legal profession for solutions. Talk to other business owners and managers about how they manage their businesses and how they approach decision making. Can you imagine a doctor's office without a system to track clients, medical history, test results and everything else? Learn from them and use what you can as you create your own solutions.

Finally, repeat this mantra as you go through this book: *process before purchase; data before decision.* Many lawyers seem to have a love-hate re-lationship with technology. Perhaps for both reasons (the love and the hate) many purchase software before properly understanding their process and evaluating their needs. Leave decisions about technology to the end. First, set firm goals, review the firm processes and consider data.

Goal Setting

Setting goals for individuals and the firm is a starting place, but these goals are by no means static, particularly if this is a first-time exercise. Unlike financial results, goals can be changed or refined as the year progresses. Goals include key performance indicators (KPIs). Please note the word "indicator" in KPI. KPI measures are meant to be reviewed and "indicate" where to focus time and attention to any necessary changes.

Goals are quantitative. For example, how much you would like to make per year? Or how much money do your clients owe you at the end of each month? And goals are also qualitative, like feedback measures, which may still be numbers, but those numbers represent a range of performance. A common qualitative measure is Net Promoter Score, which is made up of numbers that represent people who will promote your firm, be neutral, or deter others from your practice. Often Net Promoter Score is supplemented by comments and other qualitative feedback. This book is not about how to set up and manage a KPI framework or calculate these measures. I have already published a comprehensive book, *Small Law Firm KPIs,* on this topic, available at popular Internet retailers. Check it out, you will be introduced to extremely valuable measures and techniques that you can directly deploy into the strategic management of your practice.

We are going to use two firms to illustrate how to set up and keep score for some of the key measures. However, what is important is our deep dive into how to change your firm's approach and systems to ensure your clients are happy and you are satisfying your firm and individual goals.

Where to start

Often when a firm is looking to make improvements, they pick a new technology and try to implement it. However, the place to start would be uncovering your pain points or problem areas. Take a step back to analyze both your perceived problems and where you spend your time. After all this, having an implementation plan is key. Numerous examples exist where firms have tried to deploy technology but failed in the implementation. For the overall approach to making improvements or changes you can refer to Appendix B.

What is your biggest challenge?

Many attorneys I spoke to say that they are working all day and sometimes late into the night almost seven days a week - yet they do not make enough money. The 2017 Clio Legal Trends Report shows that lawyers, on average, practice law for only about 2 hours per day. Collection is the only statistic that really matters as recording hours and billing mean nothing unless the cash is received. That is a shockingly low number to those new to the practice, but not surprising to veteran attorneys.

For many the problem is described as not enough hours in the day, lack of focus, or time management. Some also say that not having enough clients can be a challenge, but the question is, if you cannot serve existing clients, why do you want new clients? Won't that just cause additional problems? And how do you know that you are serving the right clients? What defines the right client? And are you meeting those clients' needs? Are you truly able to be their advisor and advocate?

When researching for my books, I was surprised by the number of attorneys that do not use fundamental project management techniques. Not to be confused with software, these are simple time management approaches to improved productivity and apply to any setting. In our firm examples, we will share some approaches, and you can also reference the chapter below on time management.

What do you do each day?

Take thirty minutes and look back over the past ten working days. Review your calendar and your email inbox plus any lists or task management system. Do you have a set approach to each day?

Unfortunately, law school does not make for good business management training for solo and small firm owners. Compounding the problem, common attorney traits include risk aversion and a reluctance to experiment or change. Most lawyers wish to be in control and the final authority on everything. I am not recommending that you abandon those traits for your practice of law, but consider that the same approach for managing your firm may not be serving you well for client development, team compensation and firm culture.

Consider adopting the following to improve your firm management:

- *Fight the Lawyer Stereotype.* Develop a collaborative and open management style. Avoid the command and control style that is prevalent in firms.

- *Stick to your Strengths.* Not everyone is good at client development or administration; therefore do not take on impossible tasks. Ask your team for their views of your strengths and try to share the administrative load.

- *Build a Team to Compliment not to Replicate.* Understand the team's skill set when it comes to management and running a firm. Find people who can address existing shortcomings.

- *Outsource.* What you do not know can harm your firm. Therefore either outsource or delegate tasks like accounting, taxes and website development.

- *Delegate.* Again, fight the urge to control and compete by doing everything yourself. Remember: There are not enough hours in the day to do everything. By delegating tasks you cannot do or do not have time for, you not only develop your team, but you can assess others' strengths for succession planning.

Ultimately your goal is to provide value and satisfy your clients. Developing a client-centered law firm will lead to happier clients and likely a more satisfied and effective team leading to a more profitable firm.

Firm Challenges

This book is about reinventing or starting your practice so that you do not work so hard, feeling that you are falling further behind yet never achieving your goals. Once you have defined your strategic focus and ideal client you can stop trying to be all things to all clients and doing every task yourself. The best way to explain this approach is with a case study, using a completely fictitious small firm with real-life problems, identified by actual attorneys, embedded into the scenario.

Introduction to our Case Study Small Firm

Ferndale Family Law LLP (FFL) is an existing firm in Washington State whose team sits down to take stock of what's going well and what's not. Several of the team members read some recent articles on metrics and technology. The partners decided that they need to look at the flow of the work.

FFL has practiced family law for about six years as a partnership, with two partners Philip and Penelope, who founded the firm after short careers at bigger firms. Over the past several years, they have been expanding by hiring associates. Today, at the beginning of 2018, FFL employs three: Abe, Alexis, and Ashley. Abe has been with FFL the longest, almost five years and is very close to making partner.

Both Alexis and Ashley are recent law school graduates. Lisa was hired as paralegal last year to replace the previous part-time paralegal. Tim, who is a legal assistant and acts as the company office administrator, is not really trained to provide legal help. However, Tim recently graduated with a business undergraduate degree and is very enthusiastic. Particularly, Tim is keen to look at workflow because he often feels like the firm bottleneck.

Penelope attended a session at a conference last year where it was suggested that the firm assess their problems or pain points. The team set aside thirty minutes at the end of the past Monday to brainstorm their problems, challenges, or pain points.

Philip usually manages the bank accounts for the firm and views this role as a burden. He works with an accountant on the financial statements and the taxes and is always shocked by how little is left over at the end of each month. He thinks the firm needs faster collection and more new clients and perhaps should consider accepting payments online. Penelope oversees the hiring and compensation for the team and feels like she is working in isolation. Everyone complains about not having enough hours in the day to finish all their client work. Alexis is concerned that many of the clients do not understand the lawyers' workflow and their case process. She cannot take the time to explain how a case works over and over, but she worries that the clients are not happy.

For compensation, the three associates don't understand how their salaries are calculated and whether it's more important for the firm for them to bill more hours or come in under budget. Also, Alexis questions whether, with flat fees, they would need to record their hours or care about the number of hours they spend on a matter?

There was short discussion on FFL billing and fees. Most engagements are based on billing rates, but the clients always request an estimate of the potential overall time and cost. On a few occasions, clients demanded a maximum, so in effect, the matter becomes almost like a flat fee. The billing rates are raised each year, but then discounts are granted. There does not seem to be a business/profitability strategy behind FFL's commercial structure with its clients.

Challenge Framework: Cash, Clients, Compensation

Tim suggests that the problems be listed under the categories: Clients, Cash, and Compensation as follows:

Clients	Cash	Compensation
New	Faster collection	Time management
More	Flat fees?	Transparency
Faster intake	Online collections?	Firm goals?
Ideal or all?		
Expectations?		
Satisfied?		

After grouping their problems on the board, the team debates how to approach the large number of items. Philip wants to address the cash issues first and Penelope is focused on time management. Tim is frustrated with handling clients' questions and wants to focus on the faster intake.

Abe suggests that technology can solve the problems across the board and recommends seeking help from an outside consultant. Tim and Penelope both caution against jumping to technology as a solution. Lisa shares that her last firm purchased a practice management system and hired a new website designer and tried to implement everything at once. The result was chaos and because the attorneys did not have time to change their approach, most did not use the new software. Ashley and Alexis both want to learn more about time management as they have enough client work from the partners.

The partners decide to take ten more minutes to figure out the top pain point with input from the group. Penelope and Philip explain that even though the firm has been around for six years, recently they have been experiencing a lot of competition. Penelope has talked to some potential clients who have decided to go with a rival firm that uses do-it-yourself technology to reduce overall costs. Other former clients represent themselves using online, self-service forms for smaller matters. Ashley explained that some of the group and subscription legal plans are advertising that their offerings include simple family law matters. Also, Washington has introduced Limited License Legal Technicians (LLLTs). They are able to provide family law assistance but not represent clients in court. The team decides that the top pain point is new and more clients, combining the first two problems listed under the client category.

Focus on Client Challenge: New Client Process

A week later, the meeting agenda was to examine the existing steps in the process for attracting and securing new clients and look at improvements or changes to this existing process. However, the meeting was derailed before that could happen. Tim had spent about five minutes with some Post-it® notes on the whiteboard to show how they currently engage with new clients, and this sparked a completely different discussion.

Tim identified that their new clients are either coming directly through the website (contact form or call to the office main number), from referrals or from writing and speaking engagements. He also separated out former clients who are returning with new matters because sometimes he hears about those clients directly from the attorneys or more frequently, Lisa enters a new matter directly into

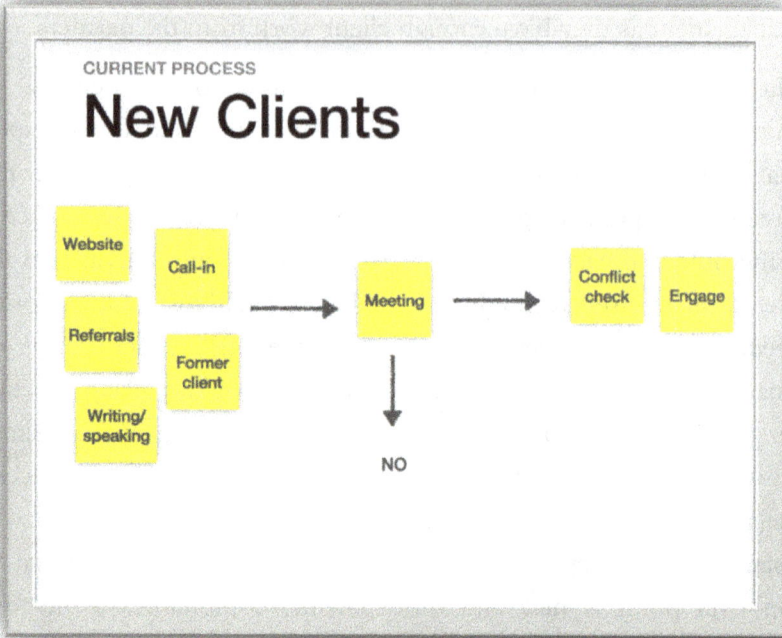

CURRENT PROCESS
New Clients

the system if the work is for an existing client. Tim is not sure if those count as new clients. Also, the referrals are all lumped together from other firms, former clients and referral agreements through approved paid channels.

Penelope writes frequently for national online publications and limited local speaking, but does not have a formal way of following up on those engagements. Philip also speaks at the local bar association and its sponsored events in the community, but he too does not have a system to capture any potential clients.

As the diagram above shows, all five new client sources lead to a meeting with an attorney, which Tim schedules. If it's a no, then there is no further action. If it is a yes, a conflict check is next, which is done by Tim. If that conflict check is okay, then Tim sends an engagement letter to start the matter.

The team realizes two things. First, even though this flow is very high level and does not contain details, it's enough to realize that Tim is doing everything, and no technology is being used to help him. His comments in the past about being a glorified scheduler or calendar czar are true. Second, the conflict check takes place after the meetings. Therefore, an attorney could waste the meeting time on someone who cannot be a client. Both Philip and Penelope are shocked that this is their new client process because it is obviously inefficient and does not make use of everyone in the office. And now it appears that Tim, despite his best efforts at scheduling meetings, could inadvertently become a bottleneck in the new client process. Tim says that he often searches for the next available attorney rather than the best match for a potential client.

However, the meeting is actually halted when questions start coming at the partners about the firm itself:

- Alexis brings up the question of whether the firm wants to take all the clients, regardless of matter. In other words, if the conflict check checks out, is that the only criteria to become an FFL client? She doesn't understand completely how the finances of FFL work, but is there a way to identify which clients are preferred?

- Ashley wants to know about targets and billable hours plus whether the firm would consider fixed fees?

- Lisa brings up the issue of having problems explaining the process to potential clients and wonders about a new package approach.

- Tim wonders if every client needs a thirty-minute meeting in person with an attorney, usually a partner.

With these broad questions, Penelope and Philip see that they need to meet to decide the firm's goals with respect to the clients they serve and the desired financial outcomes for the firm.

Takeaways:

- Identify problems or challenges first using a framework with Client, Cash, Compensation categories;

- Look at process before making any technology purchases;

- Process review can be done using just a whiteboard and Post-it® notes; and

- Involve the entire team and be transparent with firm goals.

Firm Goals

After identifying a need in the first team meeting, Penelope and Philip get together and discuss the firm's overall goals with respect to clients, cash, and compensation. When they planned the firm seven years ago, they basically wanted to make as much money as possible. Philip was in the process of leaving a mid-size firm with over a hundred partners and Penelope worked in a small firm that had twenty partners. They both found the bureaucracy frustrating and overwhelming and saw that the processes for new client approval prevented them from serving as many clients as possible.

Therefore, when they started FFL, their goal was very simple: Help as many people as possible and make as much money as possible. Since the practice opened six years ago, there has never been any follow-up collaboration to discuss the firm's goals. Each quarter, the partners met to review financial statements and billing reports but not strategy, objectives, or goals. Additionally, once a year, their accountant creates a budget that builds on the prior year. However, those metrics are not examined further, and certainly, neither partner had an answer to Alexis's question about 'ideal' clients versus serving everyone.

Philip put the following up on the board for discussion:

Our Take-Home Pay

2015	$125,000
2016	$75,000
2017	$150,000
Budget 2018	$175,000

The dip in take-home pay in 2016 was from unpaid billings for several clients, and their accountant had explained that they needed to improve collections. Last year, after changes that included doing billing within a few days of the end of the month and implementing retainers for complex matters over $50,000, the partner pay rebounded. Also, because this meeting was taking place early in the year, in January, there was still time to make changes for 2018.

Both partners laid out their goals over the next few years, including financial and client related. Penelope's goal is to work less than a full week by the time she's forty years old, which is in about five years. She would only work three days a week in the office and a half day at home. Today she works the standard five-day weeks in the office plus she works from home over the weekends. She is extremely stressed by the firm and its responsibilities. Her ultimate financial goal is an annual salary of $250,000 even with the part-time work, again by the time she's forty.

Her goal, when she started the firm, was to serve middle class and lower income clients. She never planned to take on high income or high net worth individuals. Penelope wants to create more access to justice through using either technology or paralegals, even potentially Washington's LLLTs. She hired Lisa to build her client base and leverage lower billing rates and would also like to move towards a flat fee structure. FFL does have some flat fee contracts, but only for some smaller projects. Almost all the divorces that they handle are based on billable hours.

Penelope would also like to see that the associates and other team members are compensated based on something other than billable hours. She is not sure what, but it does not seem sustainable to continue using billable hours as their compensation metric. In summary, Penelope wants growth in both clients and cash but wishes to focus on a certain client profile, streamline processes, and ultimately work less.

Philip has slightly different goals. He wants to work four days a week starting this summer and not work on weekends because of family responsibilities. His financial goal is to make a little less than Penelope, and he recognizes that if he pulls back his involvement, he will be able to take home less work. Ultimately, his goal is $200,000 per year, and again, he does have to figure out how to balance this out with Penelope.

Philip's goals include doubling the firm's revenue within three years. He wants to start using technology, and he also sees that if he delegates the work to others, the firm can make more money. He thinks that both partners are working at the wrong level and the same can be said for the associates. He agrees with Penelope's idea about changing the compensation structure so that the associates do not hoard work that should be done by Lisa. Although he was against hiring a paralegal, he now sees that they should grow that part of the firm as the revenue grows.

In addition, Philip sees that the three associates want to increase their billable hours and are also often working on tasks that can be done by Lisa or Tim. Philip also thinks that in order for both Penelope and him to work less, they should consider making one of the associates a partner this year. Philip has always focused on the higher end clientele, always working on several high-profile divorces at any given time. His goal is to grow that practice, particularly for small business owners. He does not see how those matters could be addressed with flat fees.

Both partners agree that they need to speak with their accountant about this ideal client concept from a financial point of view and also about setting flat fees. Given their financial goals, both see the need for more predictability in terms of pay and sense that having data and metrics plus understanding ideal clients will help achieve their goals.

Takeaways:

- Set regular meetings to examine firm and partner goals;

- Be transparent with partners about personal situations; and

- Be prepared to share the firm goals with the entire team.

New Client Process Revisited

Next, an hour-long meeting is set to review firm goals and focus on revising the new client process. First, Penelope and Philip present their goals to the team as follows:

- Identify Ideal Clients by March 30th, 2018

- Double Revenue by 2021

- Implement Flat Fees where possible by June 30th, 2018

- Move away from Billable Hours as a compensation measure by December 31, 2018

- Explore Technology for Efficiency by December 31, 2018

Next, the team reviews the existing process from the last meeting as shown below. Philip mentions that he has done more reading, and he and Tim would like about ten minutes to discuss data at the end of the meeting. Tim and Abe have done some pre-work on a new process and feel that they should make a few changes to experiment with a new approach. Both Penelope and Philip are quite concerned that any new client process should not be finalized until there is more information.

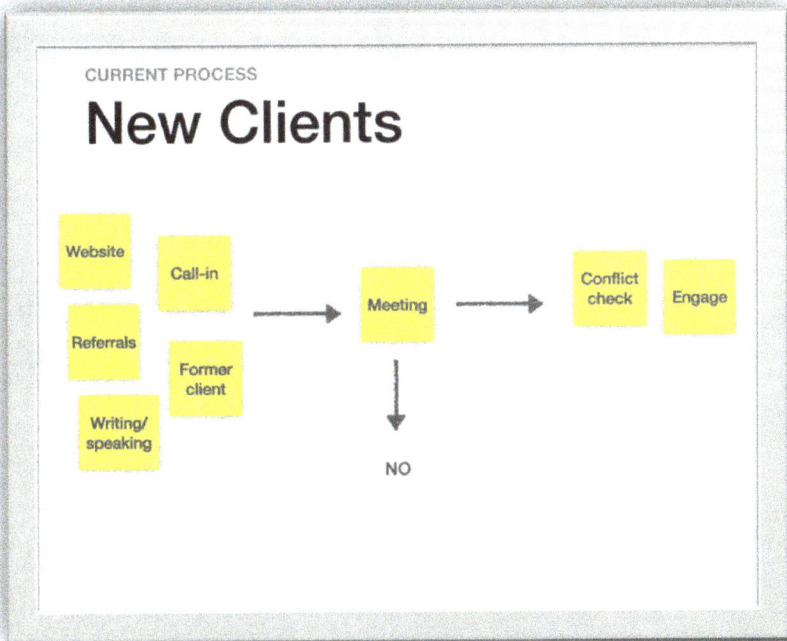

As they review the existing process, Philip comments that they should really gather data BEFORE they change anything and long before any of the technology purchases that Abe recommended. Tim reiterates that he is a scheduler for everyone. In addition, even though the meetings are all thirty minutes, because they are in person, they end up having to be blocked off in the attorneys' calendars for about an hour to allow for late starts and running over.

Philip explains that when they opened the firm six years ago, they created a website, but only recently have they spent money on search engine optimization (SEO). The company helps get FFL higher up in the websites displayed for searches made by consumers. Ashley says she has looked up the firm website on her phone, and it's hard to find the contact information because of the awkward display.

Penelope suggests that they make a list of what the issues and opportunities are with the current process so that all team members are contributing. After about ten minutes of each person individually writing their ideas to share for a quick discussion, the following list is up on the board:

- Conflict checks completed before any meetings or next steps.

- Tim is a bottleneck as he sets all the meetings and does all the conflict checks.

- Website does not show up properly on phones and tablets.

- Answering service does not book appointments

- Should all meetings be in person? Free?

- Do all clients need a meeting?

- What is the ideal client? (on the list but being addressed by the accountant and Philip next week)

- Who should do the engagement letter? Tim, Lisa, or the attorney?

- Should the engagement letter include more information on what the client can expect?

- How do more clients find them on the website?

- How do they know if the website search consultant is effective?

They decide to sketch out a new way of developing and bringing on new clients to change up the obvious flaws in the current system.

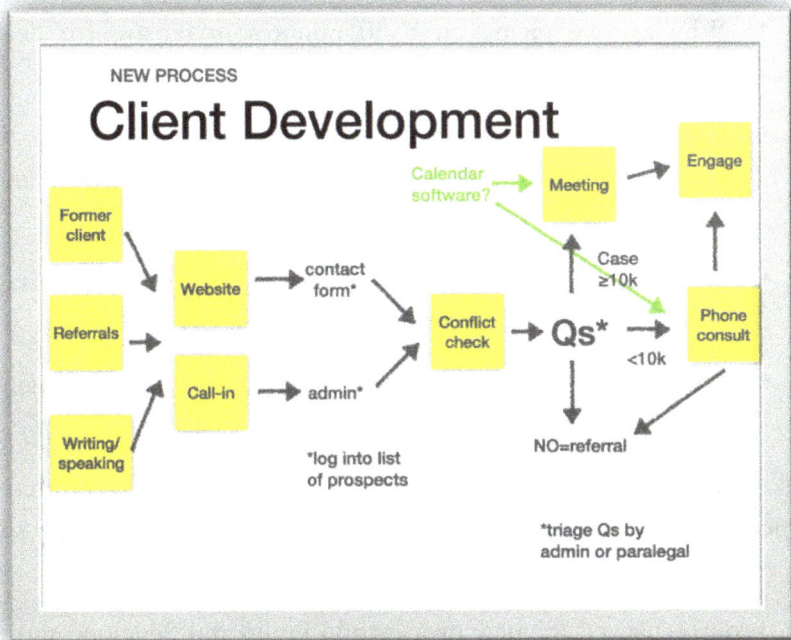

Tim had come prepared with his idea of the new process based on a discussion with Abe. They had spent about thirty minutes with some Post-it® notes to come up with the new process below.

Abe explained that it was not a particularly sophisticated session. They approached the redesign by taking the existing process Post-it® notes and re-arranging the steps and adding in the phone consultation. As they worked through the flow, the following questions came up:

- Why are the conflict checks at the end? (this question had come up in the first meeting)

- Why are all clients treated the same? Surely the same amount of time is not needed to plan for a $1,000 matter as a $10,000 matter?

- Why are we giving away 30 minutes in person for every potential client? Can we use the phone?

- Can we have a list of questions for the website and the administrator to ask to better pre-qualify potential new clients?

- Why are we not using a contact form to gather information on all the potential clients who are on the website?

- Why are we not using software to track the potential clients or their appointments?

Also, they took turns playing the devil's advocate, always, in a constructive way by just asking question such as: *Why? So, what would happen if <fill in the blank>? Does it matter if we don't do <this>?*

The group reviewed the new process and Philip and Penelope agreed to test it over the next few months without any investment in technology. Abe volunteered to create a series of up to ten questions that will help Tim or Lisa gather information on the following:

- Client and other party information for conflict check;

- The potential client's situation and perceived needs;

- Client's timeline and urgency;

- Whether the potential matter will be over $10,000; and

- Which attorney should meet with the potential client?

Ashley shared a link to a free online calendar app that works with the firm's email calendar, and she offered to show Tim how it works so they could test it out as an alternative to the current approach.

Alexis re-stated her concern that even the new process did not consider the type of client or the ideal client. Philip explained that he has a meeting scheduled with the accountant to gather the data to evaluate the ideal client from a financial perspective and committed to a review of the pricing also. The partners and attorneys are very interested in information on the source of all the potential clients.

Tim jumped in at that point to explain that he needed to gather data to better understand where the focus should be for any technology. The group agreed to give the new process a month and for Tim to gather the new data starting as soon as possible. A follow-up meeting is scheduled for early March 2018.

Data for New Client Process

One of the first questions from the partners during the session on the new client process was where do the potential clients come from? From the diagram, sources are:

- Former clients – could be current clients too

- Referrals – from other attorneys, clients and paid referral networks

- Writing or Speaking – Philip, Penelope, or other

- General Website Inquiry – fill in the contact form

- General calls – phone call

If you determine where the potential new clients come from, you can evaluate what is effective for reaching potential clients. However, it does not stop there because while these leads are important, you will want to track the lead to see if they call the firm, if they pass a conflict check and if they attend a meeting that results in a new matter.

Tim puts a blue Post-it® with the data requirements onto the new process below. The data list includes:

- Number of new inquiries by source

- Number of calls from each source

- Number of website visits by source

- Number of consultations in person and over the phone

- Number of new matters by source and type of consultation

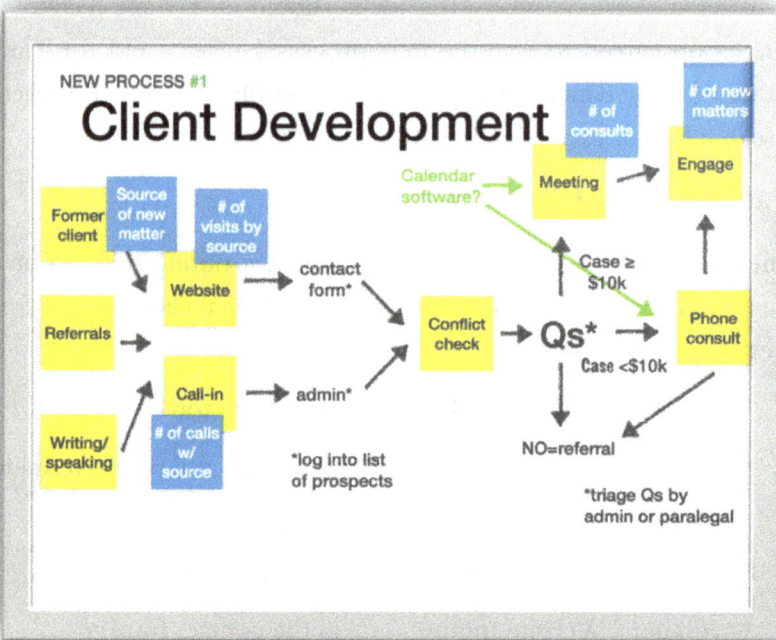

NEW PROCESS #1
Client Development

The partners gave the go-ahead for the new process without any money for technology. Tim understands that obtaining this data can be done manually and he can track using Excel. Although, you can actually use a handwritten list for data, there are software solutions, including relatively inexpensive add-on software that track potential clients as you try to convert them into clients. The key is to have one place to track everything so that there is no time wasted or errors made by moving information between systems.

At FFL, Tim has been manually tracking where each of the new clients came from when they sign an engagement letter. He asks each client how they heard of the firm at the point of engagement. However, while that data is useful, it would be much better to track each potential client from the first inquiry through the process to actual engagement. Then Tim could see at what rate the potential clients from different sources turn into actual clients. Otherwise, it's difficult to know where the focus should be on the marketing activities in terms of creating more business. Decisions like: should the firm spend more money on the internet search consultant to generate more visitors to the website; fund speaking engagements; place advertisements online or in publications; or increase the payments to the referral network?

In other words, if Tim knew that, on average, there were 25 website inquiries per week versus five calls from writing or speaking, then those data points allow a comparison between the eventual new clients and the source. If out of 25 website inquiries, there were only two new clients and, from the five presentation leads, three became clients, several tentative conclusions can be drawn, or areas flagged for further research as outlined below:

- Perhaps the website leads do not understand FFL's offerings, which can mean that the services need better explanation on the site;

- Speaking or writing allows for some pre-selling or trust building and clients have a chance to experience some of FFL's knowledge and this may be an area to expand; or

- The pricing is not shown on the website so perhaps potential clients who were interested in the firm left the site because they did not know the potential fees.

As mentioned, Tim has only a manual process for recording general data on where the client heard about FFL, and that is only for those clients that are new. Tim does not ask or record specific data if the client is a referral from past clients, current clients, or another attorney, nor does he currently record which partner or associate is their source if they attended a presentation.

Regardless of the new process, Tim recognizes that he must expand the data collected on client prospects from the website and calls. Tim plans to add "Where did you hear about FFL?" to the website contact form and also to ask callers the same questions. Tim will use an Excel spreadsheet to track the answers from the calls and website:

Where did you hear about FFL?

- I am a former client

- I am a current client

- Referral from another Attorney <insert source or leave blank>

- Referral from Network <insert source or leave blank>

- Referral <insert source or leave blank>

- I saw an advertisement

- I attended a presentation by <insert presenter>

- I read an article

- I found your firm on social media

- Other <must insert a source>

The key is to collect the answer to the above when the person first contacts FFL and continue to monitor (see New Process #2 below). This information then is used as the source data as part of the tracking of potential new clients and the number that turn into paying clients. You can record this in a complex software product called a customer relationship management system, but that is not necessary. You can start simple like Tim by using Excel or even set this up to be recorded in a notebook. The important part is to start with all the information so that you can track each source through your client marketing efforts. In addition, a list of all the potential clients can be generated to gauge the amount of upcoming work.

New Client Process Redesigned

As Tim started gathering data and working through the new client development process during the month-long experimentation phase, he realized that several additional steps and items needed to be added.

Originally, in addition to gathering more data on the source of the new clients, Tim was implementing the following changes:

- Move conflict check up in the process so that no time is wasted on clients that cannot be taken on;

- Implement Abe's triage list of questions for Tim or Lisa to complete with the potential client over the phone;

- Matters that are potentially over $10,000 should have an in-person meeting and those under $10,000 should have a phone consultation, both should be thirty minutes.

Tim noted that the sources needed to be increased to reflect existing clients; break down the three distinctive referral sources; and add advertising. Also, data should be gathered for the number of conflict checks that fail by source. To be consistent, Tim changed up the new client process flow to include the triage questions as a step after the conflict check. He also clarified that either a failure of the triage questions or the two types of meetings (in-person or phone consultation) may lead to either the client deciding not to go with FFL or

FFL declining to represent the client. At that point, FFL may refer the client elsewhere if appropriate.

For the client meetings, Tim will stop booking more than thirty minutes for the phone consultations, but will continue to block an hour for the in-person visits. Tim has done some research with help from Alexis and Lisa and discovered that some other firms are charging for upfront consultations. For the next meeting, Tim adds the other ideas

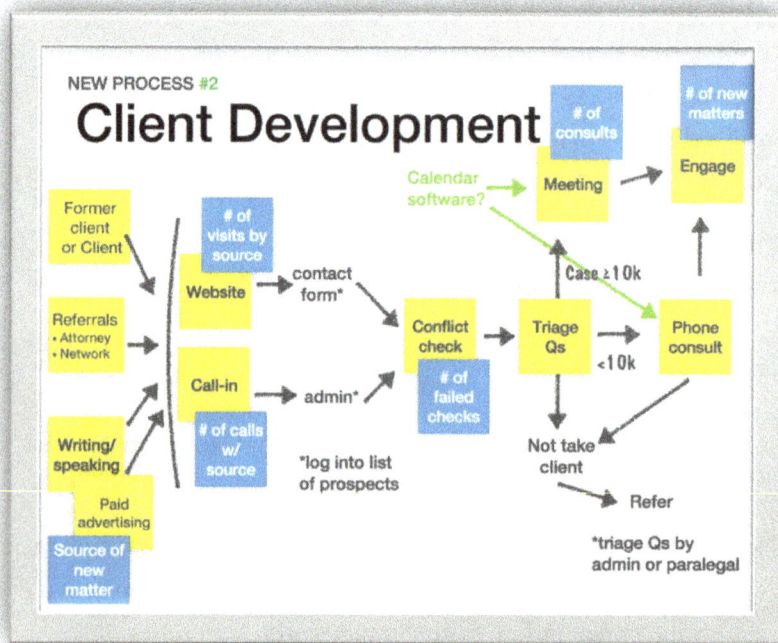

NEW PROCESS #2

Client Development

above into a second version of the new client process as shown below. He hopes to ask the partners for an experiment to be run later this year where FFL can test out a fee for client consultations.

Takeaways:

- Data is necessary to make any decisions;

- Good data starts with the source, and it's critical to keep track throughout the process;

- Process review can be done with simple Post-it® notes on a whiteboard;

- Remain open to changes when examining current processes, and learn how to respectfully ask why; and

- Don't be afraid to experiment and try new approaches.

The last two takeaways need to be highlighted. Without Tim and others questioning various steps, the client development would not be evolving. Also, the only way to test these changes is by experimenting, either with an attorney, practice area, or firm, depending on the size.

Clients: Deeper Dive into Data & Profitability

What is an Ideal Client?

In the meantime, Philip has his meeting with the accountant, Chris, who explains to him that defining ideal clients is an art rather than a science, but regardless, requires good financial data. Chris describes how the same data can be used for pricing and therefore, part of this exercise will create the foundation for any fixed fees that FFL may implement.

Philip points out that he believes there are qualitative factors that impact the experience of working with good clients. He enjoys working with certain people and, of course, wants to help others solve their problems.

Chris points out that Philip and Penelope are running a business. Chris continues by explaining that the ideal client must generate a profit. He has worked with several firms, including another business law firm, to define their ideal clients, and as a result, adjusted those firms' pricing and helped them implement budgeting.

Chris warns Philip that not only do you need the right data to evaluate potential clients, but you must be willing to say no to those that will not be profitable. Focusing the firm's efforts solely on the ideal clients will pay off in the long run rather than trying to do everything for everyone.

Chris explains that, in general, depending on the estimated length of your potential relationship with a client, you may wish to take some time with them first to ensure that it is a good fit and to analyze the numbers. If you are a business attorney, you may wish to go slow by extensively triaging or consulting first before bringing on a client that could be with you for years. Likewise, if there are problems or issues, you should not hesitate to fire clients' ethically but promptly.

How to Measure Client Profitability

A client is profitable if the revenue from their matter exceeds the costs of delivering the legal services. Chris explains that these calculations are separate from FFL's financial statements. Before you can determine client profitability, there are some calculations required to average out fees collected by matter. Often a firm has numerous offerings and will need to simplify and average out fees.

Chris has listed the services offered by FFL, in no particular order, as follows:

- Name Change
- Adoption
- Separation
- Divorce
- Alimony & Maintenance
- Custody
- Enforcement Child Support
- Paternity
- Property Division
- Modification
- Consultation

Chris created the FFL Matters by Category chart below based on analyzing financial data on the average amounts per matter *collected* over the past year. If FFL had fixed fees, he could have used those prices, if the full amounts had been collected. It's important to look at how much was actually collected as opposed to billed. This is also true for analyzing compensation, pricing and overall firm performance.

The fees are averaged out in order to compare the revenue to expenses in each category. This cannot be used for pricing without further analysis, but provides a starting point. Chris grouped the twelve FFL offerings into just five categories. However, when he saw the range of amounts in the separation and divorce categories, he realized that those needed to be broken down further because otherwise the data would be meaningless. For example, a separation agreement is four times as expensive when there are kids and a company, and a divorce is eight times more. Also, Chris shares that about 75% of FFL revenue over the past two years has come from divorce matters.

FFL Matters by Category	Average Client Fees Collected	Notes on Offerings
Separation – no kids	$2,000	Basic agreement to separate and file.
Separation – kids	$4,000	
Complex Separation – kids | company	$8,000	
Divorce – Basic no kids	$10,000	Includes Custody, Property Division, Alimony & Maintenance.
Divorce - Basic with Kids	$20,000	
Complex Divorce with Kids | Company	$80,000	For more complex, expert witnesses are billed separately at cost.
Enforcement – Child Support, Custody, Alimony & Modification	$4,000	Includes court representation if necessary.
Consultation; Child Support; Modification; Paternity; Name Change	$2,000	Miscellaneous matters that include filing but not court appearance.
Adoption	$30,000	Only two adoptions per year over past three years.

Philip reviews the chart above and is surprised by the average fees. He asks Chris to explain how he calculated these amounts. Chris provided a list of the steps so that Philip could explain to the FFL team. Chris spent several hours with the past year's timekeeping, billing and collections systems to extract the data as follows:

- *Used the past year because it best reflects FFL ongoing practice and is representative of the annual client matters.* If not, Chris would have used only that information that is most representative of the firm offerings on a go-forward basis.

- *Grouped twelve types of FFL offerings into the categories based on his knowledge of FFL business.* Again, this is where it becomes more of an art and less of a science. The goal is to have a manageable number of categories that are different from each other in terms of offerings but similar in terms of work and price.

- *Gathered the amount collected by matter from both the accounting and timekeeping billings systems.* If the firm was bigger and had a massive number of diverse offerings, Chris could have instead taken the ten largest matters and used them for an average. With FFL, Chris had to break down the categories of separation and divorce because otherwise one average revenue number for each category would have been misleading.

- *Scanned through the numbers and removed the unusual cases or outliers.* For example, Penelope and Philip together did one complex divorce for a millionaire last year, and the fees included over $50,000 for experts in addition to a fixed fee of $100,000. That is not the norm at all, and in fact, when Chris ran a quick comparison of the revenue versus the cost of the partners' time, it was close to breakeven. Although it is removed from the average, it is important to discuss separately.

- *To conclude, Chris took the* **average** *of the amounts collected by matter* **divided** *by the total matters in each category and* **rounded** *to the closest even number in thousands.* This exercise can be done by anyone, but it's best if it involves someone with a familiarity with the firm's numbers and basic bookkeeping skills. Lawyers should delegate bookkeeping and analysis to the experts.

Chris reminds Philip that preparing the FFL Matters by Category chart is not a precision exercise, and he should revisit these calculations at least once a year, if not every six months. Given that FFL is making some changes, Chris suggests review in three months using 2018 results.

Based on these results, Philip makes a note to discuss changing the threshold amount for an in-person interview to $15,000 in the new client development process. His rationale is that a basic separation or divorce consultation can be done over the phone. He would also like to consider charging for the phone consultations. Philip is worried that half an hour of time is being given away to people who may spend only $2,000. FFL billing rates range from $100 per hour for Lisa to $300 per hour for Philip and Penelope. Chris explains that the $2,000 is only an average, which means that some clients could spend less or some may pay more. And again, these calculations should not be used for pricing.

How much does this new client cost?

Chris explains that there is another data point that is important for FFL to consider before a decision is made on charging for these upfront consultation meetings or phone calls. It's critical to understand how many of these meetings result in an engagement and how much time is being spent on the meetings. That data can be used to see the value of the client development efforts.

Chris puts a quick example on the board, just making up numbers:

Total meetings per month = **40**

Number of new clients = **8**

Success rate of **20%** (8 new clients divided by 40 meetings).

Total meeting time is 20 hours at an average FFL rate of $200 per hour is **$4,000**.

So, acquiring these new 8 clients cost FFL $4,000 or $500 each, not including marketing costs. This cost is based on the assumption that the attorneys would have otherwise been spending time on billable work. Chris outlines that this $4,000 is not necessarily a good or bad number. Until FFL understands the value of the new work sold, no decision can be made as to whether that is too much or too little.

Philip explains that FFL is just starting to gather this type of information and that he will share this approach with Tim. FFL will also collect this information for each attorney's meetings with potential clients because it is more useful than just one number for the entire firm.

How much does each Category of Clients Contribute?

Next, Chris shows Philip a chart where the matter timekeeper costs are deducted from the revenue to give an amount that is left over to pay the FFL overhead costs and generate a profit. That amount is called 'contribution' which is not a buzzword, but rather an accounting concept.

The parallel in your daily life is how much you have left over after you pay the fixed mortgage and the car payments, etc. In other words, how much do you have to contribute towards your other living costs, such as your food, entertainment and cell phone bills, etc.?

As mentioned above, the calculations in this chart are used only for ideal client purposes and can be used to help with pricing at a later time. They are not reported to anyone outside FFL.

Just for background and to help Philip understand so he can explain to the rest of the FFL team, Chris reviews the FFL financial statements. At this point, only the partners receive the statements each month.

The FFL firm monthly income statement includes the following:

- **Revenue** (billings from all matters and all other sources of income);

- **Expenses or costs** (_payroll or personnel costs, partner draws_, or outside counsel or assistance on matters, plus _overhead costs_ like rent, office supplies, internet hosting, marketing, advertising, software licenses or subscriptions and professional fees, such as accounting);

- **Net profit or income** is the positive result from revenue minus expenses (a negative amount would be called a loss).

Chris then compares those statements to the FFL Contribution chart. Contribution is calculated in a similar manner by creating mini-income statements for the matters in each category _without_ deducting any overhead costs. In other words, how much is left over from the revenue for the matters in a category to contribute towards paying the FFL overhead bills, after deducting the salary costs for the people doing the work (timekeepers).

Arriving at the timekeeper costs or expenses for each matter category was a bit tricky for Chris because FFL accounting and practice management systems do not match the payroll expenses to each matter. Instead, the information gave the value of the hours by timekeeper by matter, also known as the work in progress (WIP) value by matter.

Chris was then able to work out the hours and calculated the costs based on the hours and then add in a percentage for the employee and partner payroll benefits.

An example will illustrate the calculation.

If there are ten hours in the matter that are billed at $200 per hour, the matter WIP will be $2,000. However, that $2,000 does not represent the matter expenses because FFL does not pay the attorney a salary equal to their billing rate.

Instead, to calculate the matter costs, we calculate the cost to FFL for the ten hours based on the amount paid to the timekeeper. In this example, ten hours at $100 per hour plus 30 percent for benefits (another $30 per hour) is $1300 for matter payroll costs. Therefore, with timekeeper hours by matter, you can calculate the matter expenses at this granular level and also at a higher level, using averages.

As Philip is familiar with the monthly financials, Chris put together the figures below using that complex divorce matter as an example of how to calculate the contribution from that particular matter. Chris wanted Philip to understand the approach and see the issue with this particular matter as an example.

- *Matter Revenue: $100,000*
  represents amount billed *and* _collected_ but without the experts' revenue of $50,000, which was paid by client and sent directly to the experts)

- *Matter Expenses: $95,000*
  (costs for payroll and partner draws including benefits and the direct expenses of experts that are **not billed to the client)**

- *Contribution: $5,000*
  (the amount left over or available to pay overhead costs, which is **5%** of the $100,000 of revenue)

Philip knows that the overhead costs are at least 20% to 25% of the firm's total revenue each month. Because the revenue can go up and down, it's important to look at contribution in terms of a percentage in addition to the dollar amount. Therefore, this 5% contribution is not actually enough to pay for the overhead costs of the firm. Philip now understands how he can be very busy and generating revenue, but not making enough to be truly profitable.

Chris next shows the FFL contribution chart and again warns Philip that these are based on 2017 matters only. Also, because these are averages, the actual matters could vary greatly. He suggests they assume that 40% contribution is the minimum amount that should be left over after matter costs to cover a comfortable estimate of 25% of overhead and generate a profit of 15%. Based on that, there needs to be more investigation into the highlighted numbers in the chart below that are lower than a 40% contribution to overhead.

Philip also realizes that looking at these numbers for the entire firm when there are five attorneys and one paralegal working on matters is just the beginning. At that firm-wide level, he cannot distinguish between the people or timekeeper, working on the matters. He will need to have Chris analyze this data by each timekeeper. Chris agrees to look at the top largest matters in each category and then organize the results by timekeeper for the next month. Also, Chris recommends he run a report comparing the revenue and the hours by timekeeper for all the matters in the categories with a 40% or less contribution as a separate follow-up exercise. Below are the results, with 40% or less bolded.

The bottom line is that Philip is absolutely stunned by the ideal client results and not only the low 5% contribution number from the complex divorce case. Before this meeting, going on his gut feelings, he regularly pushes for more of the high profile complex divorce cases.

Philip thought that by doing these projects, he was marketing the firm and making money. Also, when he worked on the first draft of triage questions with Tim, he actually recommended that the firm shy away from basic separation and divorce cases due to the low fees.

FFL Contribution Chart	Average Client Fees	Contribution		Notes
		Amount left over after matter costs	As a % of Fee	
Separation – no kids	$2,000	$1,000	50%	Basic agreement to separate and filing
Separation – Basic with kids	$4,000	$1,800	45%	
Complex Separation – kids | company	$8,000	$2,000	25%	
Divorce – Basic no kids	$10,000	$6,000	60%	For more complex issues, expert witnesses are billed separately at cost and are removed from the calculation
Divorce - Basic with Kids	$20,000	$8,000	40%	
Complex Divorce with Kids | Company	$80,000	$16,000	20%	
Enforcement – Child Support, Custody, Alimony & Modification	$4,000	$2,000	50%	Includes court representation if necessary
Consultation; Child Support; Modification; Paternity; Name Change	$2,000	$1,300	65%	Miscellaneous matters that include filing but not court appearance.
Adoption	$30,000	$3,000	10%	Only two adoptions per year over past three years.

In fact, last month he had been pushing Penelope to look into an adoption referral source for new work. In addition, he had asked her to have the associates look for more of the complex divorce cases. Philip now realizes that his gut feeling was wrong about the smaller matters such as enforcement, modification, consultation, etc.

He wonders if the miscellaneous matters might be an area where FFL can employ an LLLT because these matters do not go to court. He makes a note to talk to Penelope.

Chris is thrilled that Philip asks him to work on some matter budgets once he has compiled the information by timekeeper.

Philip summarizes his points for discussion at the next FFL meeting as follows:

- Review Chris's examples and both charts with the team;

- Create budgets with both hours by task and timelines for all matters except adoption;

- Discuss hiring an LLLT to work with Lisa on the smaller matters;

- Review new figures for both charts (to be prepared by Chris) in six months;

- Consider the following change in focus:

  o Do not actively pursue any adoption matters

  o Focus on Basic Separation and Divorce new clients using phone consultations

  o Review the partner staffing on the Complex Separation and Divorce matters and charge for in-person meetings; consider changing the meetings to an hour.

Case Study: Client Performance Data

In the meeting where Philip presented the information on ideal clients, both Alexis and Ashley were quick to ask how to measure whether the clients thought that FFL was the ideal firm. Immediately, Philip resisted this notion, but Penelope thought it was worth exploring in the meeting.

Lisa brought up net promoter score, which had been used at her previous firm. There, each client was presented with a short client survey that was completed either online or over the phone. The survey included net promoter score. Lisa explained that it is similar to the questions that you often receive after making an online purchase or staying in a hotel.

How likely are you to recommend <company or in this case FFL> to friends and family? Why or Why not?

Lisa explained that her previous firm had used the traditional scoring scale of 1 to 10, where 1 means that the client is not at all likely to recommend the firm, and 10 is extremely likely to recommend. Her old firm had not asked for anything other than the number and had been shocked at the results. Unfortunately, collecting this client performance data had just started before Lisa left.

Alexis had read an article about this type of measure. The calculation is quite simple. Once you have the numbers from the clients, you group them as follows:

- *Scores of 1-6* are considered *Detractors* or people who will actively warn people not to use your firm.

- *Scores of 7 or 8* are *Neutral* or people that will do nothing to recommend or warn others.

- *Scores of 9 or 10* are *Promoters* or people that will actively recommend you and sing your firm's praises to others.

The formula is to subtract the Detractors from the Promoters, while ignoring the Neutrals. Therefore, the Neutrals are left out of the calculation, but all survey information from Detractors and Neutrals should be reviewed by the firm. Philip was surprised that this scoring would not be anonymous. Lisa explained that without the source, follow-up is impossible. In general, people are happy to provide feedback and more often annoyed if their input is completely ignored.

As Lisa was explaining the system, Penelope remembered being approached by an online store after a bad experience that resulted in her giving it a low score. The company had explained that they followed up on all the poor ratings to see how they could improve. Alexis thought that if FFL was to pursue this type of client survey, it would be very helpful to have the answers to why a client would recommend or not recommend. Lisa explained that her former firm had set up a measurement framework using the small law firm key performance indicator book, which is more detailed.

Tim thought that using a simple and free online survey tool would work to gather basic feedback to start. Everyone agreed to use both questions. Ashely thought that perhaps the survey could go out with the closing letter or even ask the client to complete it if they are in the office for a final meeting.

Takeaways:

- Ideal client analysis helps with firm profitability plus pricing, particularly flat or fixed fees and budgeting;

- Data is critical to measure the contribution by different types of clients;

- Creating the analysis may require help from a bookkeeper or accountant; and

- Net Promoter Score can be an important metric for measuring your performance.

New Client Process: Updated for Experiments

About two months later, the FFL team has a meeting on the new client development process. After Philip had presented the Ideal Client figures and charts, Tim organized his data collection on new clients by source in the same categories, paying particular attention to the different types of divorces.

Also, the associates added the different types of services from the chart to the triage questions so that Tim could decide whether an in-person or phone consultation is the next step. Additionally, based on the new pricing (see the separate chapter below), Tim can now give a range of typical prices for the matter to avoid wasting both the client and attorney time if there is not a fit.

Tim has also worked on a couple of questions for the website so that the potential client can indicate what type of help he or she is looking for. He set up a dropdown menu with simple terms such as separation, divorce, alimony, or child custody. Also, there is a place to indicate whether there are kids or step-children involved and if either spouse runs their own business.

Tim has gathered the following data over the past several months on the source of the new potential client in his spreadsheet:

Source	Inquires/Calls	New Clients	%
I am a former client	20	10	50%
I am a current client	3	3	100%
Referral from another Attorney	8	2	25%
Referral from Network (paid)	45	15	33%
Referral - other	0	0	-
I saw an advertisement	2	0	0%
I attended a presentation	12	3	25%
I read an article	16	8	50%
I found your firm on social media	12	8	75%
Search online	10	3	30%

After reviewing the data, the team decides to stop all paid advertising and to start posting all the writing done by anyone from the firm on social media. Ashley volunteers to manage this new social media outreach. Also, Aaron (the new associate that replaced Abe) suggests that any presentations be written up as articles for both LinkedIn and social media. Tim will look into the online search results in more detail, and with more data, recommend whether the website search consultant continues.

Below is version #3 of the client development or marketing approach. The marketing label was added for Aaron. This version includes paid in-person consultations and the threshold for the in-person meeting was increased to $15,000. The paid consultation is at the regular partner or associate client rate as they wish to make sure potential clients can pay FFL rates. Philip thinks that it is worth trying to implement this change to paid consultations and deducting that consult fee from the final bill for all matters under $20,000. Also, phone consultations have been reduced to 15 minutes because a lot of the information is now gathered through the triage questionnaire. Those phone calls will remain free.

Lisa worked with the associates to pull together some standard wording, which describes each of the offerings. It is used during the

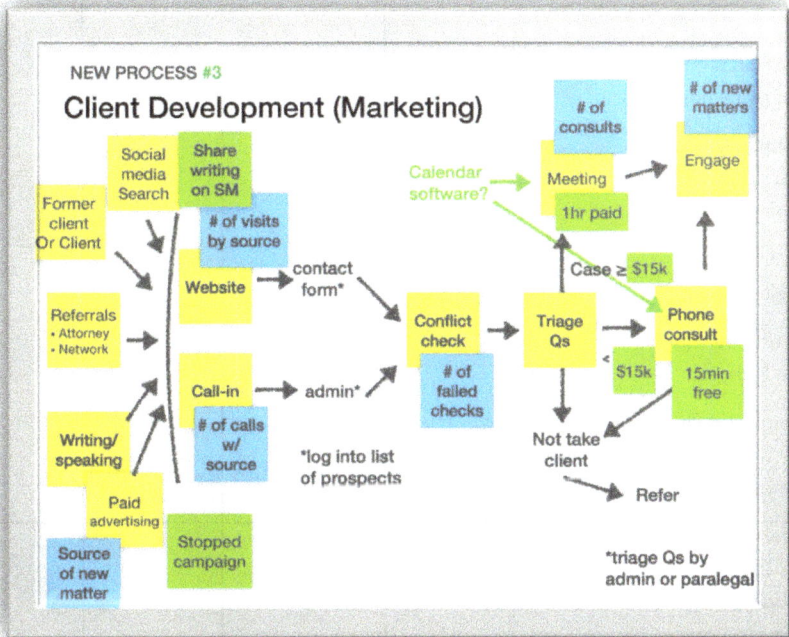

triage questions and the first meeting to manage client's expectations.

The partners give the go-ahead for Tim and Lisa to research a system to log in the prospects so that everyone can see the information. Alexis asks if that system can somehow transfer the information to the practice management system to save everyone time. Also, Tim has now convinced the partners to use the free calendar plug-in to allow for current clients to book appointments directly to their calendar. This will free Tim up to triage the new potential clients using the list of questions.

Tim will be collecting the following data over the next two months, in an Excel spreadsheet, with the goal of testing the changes made.

Categories of Potential New Matter	Type of Potential New Matter	Source	Type of Consultation	Attorney	Fee Quoted
Separation – no kids Separation – Basic with kids Complex Separation – kids | company					
Divorce – Basic no kids Divorce - Basic with Kids Complex Divorce with Kids | Company					
Enforcement – Child Support, Custody, Alimony & Modification					
Consultation; Child Support; Modification; Paternity; Name Change					

There will never be a final version of the new client development (marketing) process as the team will continuously refine the approach as more data is gathered.

Takeaways:

- Plan regular process experiments for a set period of time and measure the impacts of the changes;

- Data collection is part of the process and must be supported, but does not automatically require a sophisticated system; and

- Changes are part of the natural evolution of a business, and therefore, regular meetings to review each process should be scheduled throughout the year.

Firm Cash Management

FFL is a business and, as such, needs cash to operate. A few months ago, in the first team brainstorming meeting, a method for faster collections was at the top of the Cash column. Penelope has been doing some reading on collection metrics and has brought the following data to the team meeting based on a report provided by Chris last week.

Total Client Accounts Receivable	$500,000	100%
Current	$175,000	35%
Over 30 days	$25,000	5%
Over 60 days	$100,000	20%
Over 90 days	$75,000	15%
Over 120 days	$125,000	25%

The meeting is taking place on a Friday, with Chris in attendance, and the month end billings were done the previous week. This $500K is a very large number, more than double the usual monthly billings. Given that most of the firm's bills are due within the same month, having aged receivables for more than four months means that the firm likely will use its line of credit to pay the bills.

The team brainstorms ideas to collect money faster as follows:

- *Use Retainers.* Use retainers for all separation and divorce work. Each month's bill can then be immediately paid by the retainer.

- *Look into Evergreen Retainers.* Check into whether the Washington State Bar rules allow for the retainers to be automatically replenished.

- *Collect fixed or flat fees upfront.* Penelope will check the bar regulations. FFL has a better idea of the average size of the matters and will develop fixed fees to be paid in advance of the work.

- *Accept checks, credit cards, Automated Clearing House (ACH) and online payments.* The partners agree that online payments do not count as a technology improvement as they can simply add in an industry accepted credit card processor through their existing practice management system.

- *Assign follow-up responsibilities for client money.* At this point, only Philip receives the list of amounts owed by clients once a month. Each responsible attorney will now follow up with their own clients for receivables each week, rather than monthly. Not every client will be called weekly, but this allows for the attorneys to work on collections over the month, rather than all at once. Philip will have Chris send out a list each Monday for calls or emails.

The team had a serious discussion on why lawyers seem to be reluctant to implement collections procedures. Chris has often remarked that he is amazed that lawyers are unwilling to even call to ask for payment for completed work. In comparison to other professions, it is very odd that often entire matters are completed without the client paying.

Also, Tim realizes that currently he waits until the end of the month to run the pre-bills for each responsible attorney. Instead, he thinks that the billing should be done as soon as a matter closes that month, which should make for quicker billings on the smaller matters. Philip agrees, particularly as he thinks back to the ideal client information, which showed how much those smaller matters contribute to the firm's profitability.

A decision is made: client receivables will not go over 30 days. Also, a partner will be involved if the amount exceeds 60 days. Online payments are now the industry standard, and when coupled with timely billings, upfront fixed fee payments and retainers, FFL should see an improvement in cash position.

Collections

Today, 65% of the total $500,000 receivables ($325,000) has been outstanding for more than 30 days.

Penelope and Philip commit to spending an hour per week collecting their three largest receivables from clients and ask each attorney to apply that same policy to their matters. Bottom line is each attorney is responsible to ensure payment for their matters. Tim suggests sending out an email to all clients once the credit card processing is set up to let them know that they can now pay online. Also, the partners can speak with all clients with receivables over 90 days to see if a payment plan over several months is needed.

Penelope thinks that Chris should also indicate on the report which clients are still active and those need to be addressed first rather than just the three largest amounts. Philip agrees the list should be sorted by the largest and active clients.

Alexis suggests that weekly numbers be circulated on the progress toward recovering the $500K in receivables. The other associates agree, but Ashley questions how this will impact their billable hour targets. Penelope is quick to explain that the compensation structure is being reviewed, and with a move towards fixed or flat fees, things will change. She also explains that there will be a meeting to present the new plan for feedback from all.

Budgeting

With all the changes going on, Philip and Penelope decide to update the 2018 budget because they were a bit lazy last December when they originally prepared it. Philip asked Chris to increase revenue 10%, spread equally over the year, and to keep the expenses the same as the 2016 budget. The plan is no changes in staff other than giving the associates the regular step up to the next year's salary and a small increase for Tim. Lisa is a new hire, therefore no increase was planned until 2019.

Chris has advocated the budgeting approach that starts with a clean slate every year, followed by calculating monies needed for partner take-home pay and work backwards. Also, Chris suggested that once the firm budget is complete, it should then be used to create targets for all the timekeepers, and all matters have budgets for both effort and timelines. Now that Philip has seen the results from the ideal client exercise, he is eager to implement more refined budgets.

Below are the steps to improve the 2018 budget as recommended by Chris as the firm's accountant.

Firm Revenue

The partners will look at what can be generated from the team based on 2017 results plus their proposed partner draws and the firm expenses. Those numbers will change each month depending on which timekeepers are available. Therefore, Philip will gather the vacation schedules for everyone for the remainder of the year.

The 2018 goal is to work on fixed and flat fees so that, for 2019, the budget for each type of matter can be calculated in addition to the monthly revenue targets.

Firm Expenses

Penelope and Philip take an hour and go line by line through the 2017 monthly expenses to see what is still needed and where increases are required. They realize that they had just rolled over a large office supplies budget that was not used last year. However, their internet hosting bill has increased because they were over budget last year and have not yet adjusted. Overall, the expenses were reduced by about $40,000 based on their review.

The partners decide to put that same amount in a bonus pool for the rest of the team. In addition, both partners submit their monthly draw figures for the full year to help Chris create the expense and revenue plan.

Timekeepers & Matters

Let's take a step back from the FFL story to the time when I practiced as an accountant, way back in the last century before online timekeeping. We were given a budget for each company's audit by section. We recorded our time manually on a pre-printed timesheet for each of those sections. Every week we would receive a budget versus actual progress report broken down by those same sections. Even in those days, our audits were flat fee engagements.

My first summer, I blew the budget on an accounts receivable section because there were many strange balances, which threw off my samples and needed to be investigated. My instinct was to not record the extra time on my timesheet because I wanted a good evaluation. My supervisor told me, in no uncertain terms, that inaccurate reporting would hurt the firm for several reasons:

- Any chance of recovering that extra time spent in the form of additional billings would be lost forever;

- Future budgets would be incorrect because the time was not captured;

- Understanding how much time was spent is important for the firm to potentially change their flat fees; and

- In this case, the reason for the extra hours was on the client's side, but if I had been unable to complete the work within the budget because of my own shortcomings, the firm could then identify the need for additional training.

Although my experience was in a different country, century, and profession, it's transferable to FFL. In fact, FFL's accountant Chris recommends the approach in the bullet points above to the partners. FFL will continue to capture the hours worked on all the projects, including non-billable time. In addition, the partners agree that hours will no longer be the driver for the timekeeper's salaries.

Takeaways:

- Cash is the lifeblood of the firm and therefore a basic understanding of firm finances and budgeting is critical at the partner and also associate level;

- Regular budgeting can assist with pricing; and

- Tracking time is still essential even if a firm is not billing by the hour because it provides valuable data.

Compensation

When the FFL team met to discuss problems, the associates were concerned about the transparency of the compensation, and Penelope was worried about working on the hires and salaries in isolation. As outlined above, the partners committed to transparency around a new plan that will be phased in over 2018.

Partner Compensation

You may have seen charts that compare the take-home pay for solo or small firm attorneys to those that work in BigLaw. For example, Glass Half Full: The Decline and Rebirth of the Legal Profession includes charts on solo versus big law partners. I would not waste time trying to make these comparisons. Without getting into too much detail, I think a quick example can explain the difference that occurs because the studies often use information from the tax returns after the owners' deductions.

Let's compare take-home dollars, using fictitious data for a partner draw of $100,000 versus a salaried attorney who earns the same.

Partner | Owner
Draw $100,000

Deductions (on tax return)

$30,000 car lease

$20,000 home office deduction

$10,000 meals, travel, and entertainment $ 60,000

Income to be taxed at 25% $ 40,000

Tax $ 10,000

Employee Attorney

A $100,000 salary would be reflected as wages on a tax return, and the attorney would then pay taxes at the personal rate before having money to pay for their car and other expenses.

Salary $100,000

Tax @ 25% $ 25,000

As owners, Philip and Penelope have the benefit of tax deductions that a salaried lawyer who receives a regular paycheck and a W2 for tax purposes does not.

Rather than worrying about statistics and what other attorneys show on their tax returns, the two partners have defined their personal cash needs and passed on that information to Chris.

Team Compensation

FFL has used a lock-step grid for its associates since inception. Penelope has simply moved the associates through the grid without much input from Philip. The billable hour targets for each associate year decrease over the years as the attorneys take on more pro-bono work and client development responsibilities. Penelope has not really focused on those hour targets as measures of an associate's performance and has given mainly anecdotal feedback. This has led to some angst amongst the associates because they are not clear on how compensation works.

Penelope and Philip decide to revamp the salaries and add in a bonus.

Most importantly, they wish to make the compensation system more transparent for all the timekeepers plus align with the firm goals and individual metrics. Alexis had questioned whether the number of hours should really be important, given that FFL is moving to flat or fixed fees.

Philip explained that the actual number of hours should still be recorded in order to create accurate budgets and pricing. However, the partners are focused on satisfying the clients and collecting fees, therefore billable hours are no longer a compensation metric.

The changes to the system are presented to all timekeepers, including Tim, as follows:

- Metrics no longer include billable hours, but instead are based on revenue generated and collected by the timekeeper.

- Completing matters on a timeline will be measured as will the actual time spent on the matter versus the budget. The latter will be reviewed for future pricing and budgeting, but the focus is delivering services to clients on-time.

- The new net promoter score results from clients will also be factored into performance.

- The number of successful client consultations will be included in performance evaluations.

The new bonus will be comprised of a combination of firm performance and individual results. Once that simple calculation is created, it will be shared with everyone at FFL. Penelope has created a small committee that includes Ashley, Tim and Lisa to work on this plan for the firm.

Pricing

The old school approach means that FFL would look at the competitors' billable hour rates and set the hourly rate in the same range. Clients are demanding predictability with respect to their legal bills in all matters, personal and corporate. Therefore, continuing to offer services on a billable hour basis is not client-centered, and FFL wishes to move from rates to flat or fixed fees.

What about billable hours?

If you would like your firm to still use billable hours, you can use the same type of average fee analysis to calculate how much to bill for each type of matter. For example, if you can be profitable charging $10,000 for a matter, and you estimate that matter will take 40 hours, the billable hour rate should be $250. However, clients must be willing to pay that rate.

Another approach is to work backwards into a rate based on how much annual revenue you need to generate and how many hours you are willing to work. Please see below.

As a solo attorney, Abe is not sure how much to charge his clients yet as his firm is new. He wishes to take home $100,000 per year. He is willing to work 1000 hours per year. If he divides the $100,000 by 1000 hours, that is $100 per hour. However, that is not his hourly rate because he has not included anything for the matters' expenses or the firm's overhead. One common approach would be to double the $100 to cover the government taxes (self-employment or other), matter expenses and firm overhead, which would then result in a billable hour rate of $200. That may not be a competitive rate; therefore, a more detailed analysis should be done to work out his exact costs.

Next, divide that dollar amount by the number of hours you will be working and billing.

For example:

Abe take-home pay	$100,000
Matter expenses that cannot be passed onto client	$ 4,000
Firm overhead (software, insurance, website)	$ 46,000
Total	$150,000

In this case, instead of $200 per hour, we arrive at $150 ($150,000 divided by 1,000 hours) as the hourly rate that Abe plans on billing. Again, Abe will need to check if that rate is competitive and if clients will pay that rate.

Fixed or Flat Fee Calculation

The first step is to group similar types of offerings in terms of effort and timelines and then calculate the average fee collected based on prior years' numbers. This exercise is similar to the ideal client chart calculation and any unusually large or small cases or matters completely outside the norm should be removed from the data.

Much of the work for a fixed or flat fee structure was done by Chris for the FFL ideal client analysis. These categories and average fees were a good starting point for the flat fees. Since the time of the initial presentation of the average fees, Chris and Philip do further analysis and decide to create some variations in the smaller offerings plus increase the flat fees in a few of the separation and divorce matters (bolded below).

Penelope is in the process of hiring an additional paralegal and an LLLT for the smaller matters and also to help support the complex cases. After she and Philip reviewed the ten largest complex cases plus the one $100K outlier, they realized that they are not properly delegating work to the associates. In turn, because Lisa is the only paralegal, the associates do not delegate much either. Also, Alexis explained that she never wanted to give up billable work to anyone because she thought they had to hit their billable hour targets.

Categories	Average Fees (from Ideal Client Analysis)	Flat Fee	Notes
Separation – no kids	$2,000	$2,500	Basic agreement to separate and filing
Separation – Basic with kids	$4,000	$5,000	
Complex Separation – kids | company	$8,000	$12,000	
Divorce – Basic no kids	$10,000	$10,000	For more complex, expert witnesses are billed separately at cost and are removed from the calculation.
Divorce - Basic with Kid	$20,000	$20,000	
Complex Divorce with Kids | Company	$80,000	$80,000	
Enforcement – Child Support, Custody, Alimony & Modification	$4,000	$2,000 / $4,000	Includes court representation if necessary. Small | Regular
Consultation; Child Support; Modification; Paternity; Name Change	$2,000	$1,500 / $2,500	Miscellaneous matters that include filing but not court appearance. Small | Regular

The above flat fees must be tested from the client's perspective and adjusted as necessary. Chris will set up quarterly reports to compare budgeted time versus the actual recorded time.

A final note on recording hours. Some attorneys only use contingency fees and do not want to track time. I do not necessarily agree with this approach as the hours can be useful for estimating staffing needs. In other words, time can be used for calculations other than productivity.

Even if your firm is focused on case timelines or the number of client interactions, rather than hours, you still need to know how long each matter will take for scheduling your staff's time and setting realistic timeframes.

Also, I have seen some articles on value pricing that indicate that hours do not need to be tracked. I believe that not only does the time recording help with the budgeting and calculating of the profitable matters, but it can also help with time management as we will explore in a later chapter.

Takeaways:

- Cash is king and key to your success, therefore measure and reward based on collections, not billings;

- Align compensation with firm goals; and

- Data for ideal client evaluation is also important for pricing and budgeting. And again, tracking time is still essential even if a firm is not billing by the hour because it provides valuable data.

Keeping Score

Most lawyers that I know are inherently competitive. Actually, most professionals are goal-driven and thrive in an environment with targets. With the common goal of firm success, keeping score of firm progress can actually bring the team together. The critical piece is to make sure that the personal targets align with the overall firm goals. Additionally, the compensation system must be consistent with both firm and individual goals.

I used to think that the case or practice management systems should create the ultimate one screen, or one-page display, of all relevant data. That display or dashboard would be used to make decisions and track progress against goals. However, I am not sure if that is possible. I think it's better to create your own firm dashboard or scorecard over time. It can be as simple as using a whiteboard and markers with basic products like Excel and Word. Or you can purchase advanced software that links systems and produces a graphical scorecard.

Like any other technology, my advice is to go slow and start simple. A popular and inexpensive way to link data from different systems is Zapier.com. Also, AirTable and Zoho Reports are both less expensive dashboard software than Tableau. This is an area where it is a good idea to delegate tool selection to someone with the requisite knowledge or outsource to a technology specialist once you wish to invest in a dashboard.

Time Management

Your time is finite so use it well. Every day, we all have to manage limited resources, regardless of our profession. Almost all the attorneys I speak to cite time management as one of their largest challenges. And most then follow up with a comment about the double-edged sword of technology and constant connectivity; you are expected to be available at all times.

As mentioned earlier in the book, I believe that if you can plan a party or wedding, you have the skills to run your practice and manage your time, potentially without complex and expensive software. The key to time management is not just listing and prioritizing your tasks, but thinking about how you are impacting others' progress with your choices.

Each day when I evaluate what I need to accomplish, I ensure that I flag the items that require others' input or that others' need to get their work done. The analogy to party planning is that I must review and approve the guest list before the invitations can be sent out. If I leave that task too late, I am holding up others' progress. Therefore, I mark those tasks that impact others to be addressed first.

Project management is at the core of all success—from Post-it® notes to project management software solutions—it's more about discipline than tools because you can ignore any system. If you are constantly battling deadlines or feeling overwhelmed on a regular basis, ask yourself where you went wrong. Did you miss a reminder, did you not plan enough time, did you try to do it all yourself? Getting to the root cause of your challenge is the first step toward taking control of your time and professional life.

First, list what you planned to do and what happened for a couple of days during your last work week. Make sure to record whether you feel like you accomplished your goals on those days. For example, did you block out time for client work and get distracted on something else? Did you find that three hours went by and you were still answering emails and organizing your day? Did you accomplish all the critical tasks for the day?

The second step is planning. Consider how you would approach the project of painting a room. For those of you who have not painted, you spend more time planning and prepping than actually painting. Thus, review your approach to a regular day at work asking: How do you plan for your time? How do you monitor that plan or make changes? How do you reduce your stress level at work? Understanding the answers to these questions can help you design the best approach.

Next, find the system that works for you. We are unique individuals and what works for managing my time may not work for you. Test out various systems or approaches until you achieve your goals. And, as always, keep it simple to start and move to technology only after refining your approach.

Below are some tips and approaches to better time management from other attorneys, professionals and from my life experience. Again, it's all about how it fits with the way you approach work. Find what works for you and just do it.

- *Basic List*—start the day making a list of all your tasks and prioritize them based on client deadlines; delegate as much as possible and remember to consider if you're holding anyone else up by putting off that task. This list can be manual: a legal pad, Post-it, whiteboard, or even the wall (see Wall of Pain idea below). Alternatively, the list can be online using smart phone notes, calendar as tasks, project management system and so on. Personally, I still enjoy the satisfaction of crossing off tasks on a piece of paper. On really unproductive days, I make new lists with some old items to be able to cross them off!

- *Do daily triage*—start the evening before, make your list of critical tasks and rank them in order of attack for the morning. I make manual lists using pads of paper for overall day's items and Post-it® notes for details. I have tried to go paperless, but it makes me crazy not to be able to physically crumple up that paper. Go with the level of technology that fits you.

- *Email as To Do List (Zero Inbox)*—use your email inbox as a to-do list, and file or archive the emails as you address or resolve them. Most email systems allow for marking unread or adding flags so that at a glance you can prioritize your tasks using your inbox. However, you must first achieve zero inbox to use your email as a task list. Some people delete the emails once they reply, but I am not a fan of deleting because I have often needed a past email for information or follow-up. I have a set of folders and frequently use the search function based on person or key-word.

- *Time Block (including morning or night shift)*—actively block time for tasks. It sounds simple, but in today's connected world it's often difficult to turn off electronic distractions. Last summer while writing under a deadline, I would block out time in my calendar without meetings and actually turn off the internet at my residence. That is quite extreme, but you can disengage from your network or turn off the notifications, etc. At a minimum, if you are trying to focus on a client project or business development, turn off your email and put your phone out of reach. However, if you are trying to clear out your email, often a shift during the early morning hours or late night can allow you to plow through the inbox. Finally, check out the auto-archiving features on your email to save time.

- *Double Up: Calendar / Screen*—if you have the resources, having two monitors or screens going at once, one for the work and one for your calendar and your time keeping, etc., can make time recording and staying on schedule easier. Also, some attorneys with assistants have important deadlines calendared on both their system and on an assistant's calendar. Some even have the assistant remind them by email.

- *Wall of Pain*—an attorney that I went to law school with created her "wall of pain," which has all her professional commitments as projects broken down into tasks on a wall at her home office. In addition to client legal work, she speaks, blogs, writes and volunteers, so she needed a visual of it all. Borrowing from our color-coded highlighter law school days, she has used a different color for each task. Each day she puts a black star on those tasks that need to be done by the end of the day. For more on this approach, see the bibliography. I would add that it may also be helpful to flag those tasks that can be delegated and/or will hold up others, perhaps with double and triple stars.

- *Tasks as Calendar Appointments*—some electronic calendar systems and practice management systems have tasks that can be listed, but instead, you can add the tasks as actual meetings or calendar appointments. Using those automatic calendar reminders that appear in your email throughout the day will help keep you from forgetting important tasks. However, if your inbox is already overloaded this may not work for you as the reminders will be lost.

- *Robot Reminders*—some attorneys like to work with various intelligence personal systems like automated home systems (Alexa) or phone (Siri). Group collaboration platforms like Slack can also manage tasks plus some more sophisticated practice management systems will have calendars that can issue reminders.

- *Project Management System*—although we recommend not jumping to a software solution, depending on the size of your practice, you may wish to adopt a project management system. From a high-level perspective, project management software will help you view all your matters within the overall workflow, which is very useful for the leader of the project or firm. A project management system is different from practice management system. It's easiest to think of it as the difference between a detailed day by day set of documents and costs for your annual week-long vacation (practice management) and an overall route map showing your progress each day (project management). Your practice management software has all the information on each matter and includes your time, work product, and other client data. A project management system shows, often on one page or view, where all the matters are in the work flow. Custom colors can be used to highlight priorities on your view; it's like a digital version of the "Wall of Pain" approach. Two popular options are Trello and Asana, but try them before you buy to ensure that you and your team are comfortable using this approach.

- *Process Charts*—by setting aside time to regularly review and chart firm processes, you will design a complete system for your daily tasks. Some attorneys review all the processes at once and others stagger it throughout the year. Involving others in a regular review may uncover opportunities for delegation, simplification and time-savings.

- *Availability Expectations*—announce your expectations using the out of office function for lengthy absences or put your working hours in your signature. I know several attorneys who are transparent with clients about not working on weekends or even certain days of the week.

- *One-touch*—this is a concept that I learned in the 1980s, and the idea is to only touch the paper in your inbox once. In other words, immediately deal with any issues or actions resulting from that paper after you first read it. Translated to this century, try not to skim your emails, reading one and moving onto the next without any action. I find it almost impossible to truly apply this concept to email, but I do try to deal with emails that will only take less than a minute: Make quick introductions, ask or answer questions or delete.

Regardless of your comfort level for time management automation, remember to triage your tasks and to constantly look at where things are getting stuck and why. Lawyers are not taught to work in teams nor delegate. Effective delegation is a key skill worth learning and will help to better manage your time. And lastly, focus on your task at hand with 100% of your attention as there is no such thing as multitasking.

Takeaways:

- Time management techniques can be borrowed from other professions; and

- Tracking your metrics can be done simply without sophisticated technology, particularly in the beginning.

Case Study: Startup Solo Firm

We dove deeply into the client development or marketing workflow for FFL, but we will now use former FFL associate Abe's brand new solo firm to illustrate all the processes. The same steps that FFL took to examine firm goals, problem areas and the client development process - all are part of an overall approach (see Appendix B) that can be applied to any of these systems in a solo or small law firm at any time.

In the spring, when Philip broaches the subject of partnership, Abe decided that he's not as interested in family law as he originally thought. Abe did some work for an FFL client who was recently divorced and had founded a start-up. After the divorce was finalized, she asked Abe if he could help with some of her start-up issues. Abe has a background in business law and intellectual property from his undergraduate and law degrees. He went into family law because he found the job at FFL right out of school as their first associate. Abe decides to start his own practice as a solo helping start-ups and small businesses. He leaves FFL on good terms and agrees with Philip that they can do mutual referrals.

Abe wants to design his new firm from scratch rather than replicating the FFL work flow. He meets with Chris to ask his advice before he sits down and sketches out the way that he wants his firm to operate.

Chris outlined that the main processes in any firm can be broken into these five workflows:

- Client Development (or marketing)

- Client Intake (starting with engagement letter onwards)

- Legal Services Delivery (creation of work product, representation, all things practice of law)

- Billing and Collections (and financial reporting)

- Close & Measure Client Satisfaction (client feedback and closing engagement)

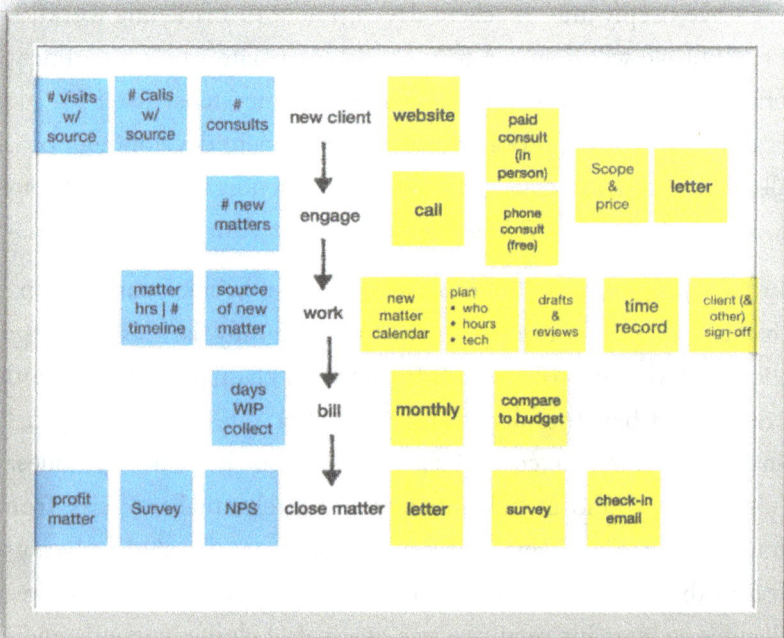

Abe lists his processes and creates a whiteboard with these listed vertically:

- New Client; Engage; Work; Bill; Close Matter

He then adds to the board as follows:

- Yellow Post-it® notes: the basic steps required for all of processes

- Blue Post-it® notes: the data that needs to be gathered to make decisions on any changes to the processes.

A fellow solo attorney let Abe know about the Post-it® Plus App. Abe used his iPhone 6 to capture the map of his processes using Post-it® notes on his wall and converted it to digital using the free Post-it® Plus App. He can then move around the Post-it® notes digitally as he creates processes and makes changes. More information is available at post-it.com/app and the output from the app is in Figure 1 below.

Figure 1: Post-it® Plus App

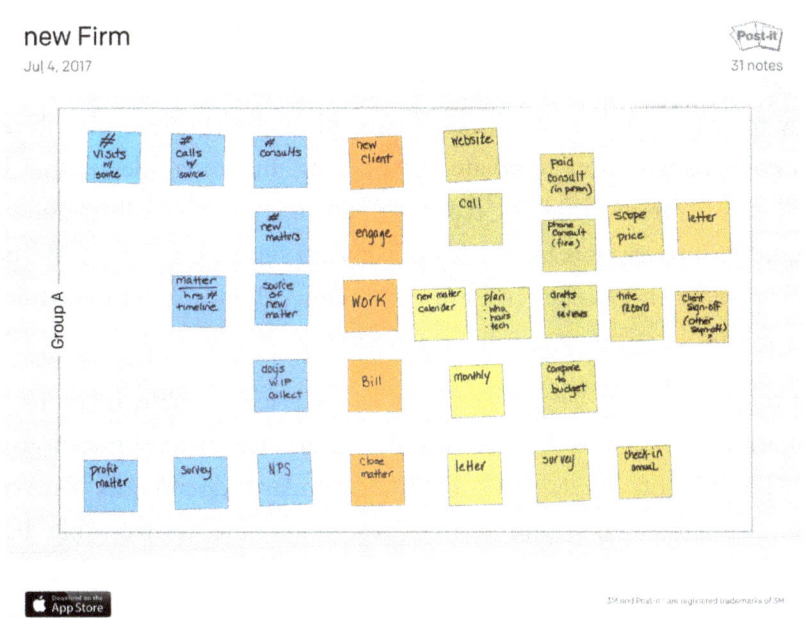

Another friend let Abe know about a flowchart software that can also be used to create a digital version of his firm's processes. Abe will hold off on that purchase because the firm is just him and money is tight. Abe read about performance measures in the Small Law KPI book and will be setting up a simple Excel spreadsheet for five indicators to start.

After Abe worked out his workflow, he decides that he will create an online law firm. His plan is to use an office at his home or in a nearby co-working space. He understands the need to detail the case steps or workflow prior to purchasing any technology (more on that in the next chapter).

As he maps out his processes, he puts himself in the shoes of a new client and walks through what that new client would experience. For example, even though he is trying to attract clients through the website only, Abe will have the ability for people to call and email him.

Next, he decides to offer only paid consultations after using technology to triage the best potential clients. Once he engages, he will use an engagement letter template. For pricing, his initial idea is that he will have three different types of pricing, which will include a monthly subscription fee for list of start-up services, a flat fee by specific project and a retainer fee for billable work hours. He will collect the money in advance as much as possible from day one.

At this point, he is basically offering any service possible: from incorporation to setting up policies; creating articles of incorporation or LLC operating agreements; drafting standard documents like co-founder agreements; and dispute resolution. He realizes that he'll need help for intellectual property matters. He will develop referral arrangements with another attorney who specializes in patents and an attorney that specializes in softer intellectual property. It's a very broad approach, but he will see which matters or services are the best from both a financial and enjoyment perspective.

Abe realizes the need to calendar and track his work including filings and any court dates. Although he is not sure if he will buy a practice management system to start, he is leaning towards something to help with calendaring, matter management and billing. But he also wants a solution for project management and budgets.

Being a solo, Abe needs to figure out how he can get all of this work done within the limited number of hours in the day. For billing, he's hoping to set up the majority of his matters as flat fees so that he can bill each month without calculations, and if he does a project matter based on billable hours, he's going to bill as soon as the project is complete.

Based on a discussion with Chris, Abe will record his time because he needs time information for pricing his matters in the future. He is offering almost every legal service possible while his practice is new, but his ultimate goal is to determine which clients are the most profitable and the ones that he can help the most. For Abe, it is not all about the money.

His plan is to gather data for the first six months and determine which clients are ideal. Abe will then focus his marketing efforts on attracting those ideal clients, mainly through writing, speaking and using social media. He will market to the startup incubators and accelerators nearby. Because he's been in practice for a few years, Abe will apply to be a referral attorney for some of the legal services providers or plans. This will cut down his marketing costs, so he can just deliver legal services. Lastly, while closing an engagement, Abe plans to include net promoter score as part of a quick exit survey. He will post any positive testimonial responses on his website.

Abe's process whiteboard, pictured above, is very high-level because he's the only person at the firm. His next step is to figure out the best technology for his practice and make him efficient. He has listed the data needed and is reminded of discussions at FFL; the data is only as good as the system or the process that creates it. If he gets the wrong information, for example, from his website analytics, he could make a bad decision on marketing spend.

Abe's biggest concern as a solo is that he will spend too much time developing new business and not enough hours actually practicing law. Therefore, he will record all hours to evaluate his marketing efforts. Next, Abe turns his focus to technology that will automate his marketing and will free him up to practice law.

Takeaways:

- The same approaches can be used for process review and data collection in both a solo firm and a small law firm;

- The types of processes are also the same for all firms; and

- Collecting data from day one will simplify process review and experimentation.

Change & Technology

Before we dive into Abe's new firm as an example of how to evaluate technology, it's important to understand the overall approach to technology implementation. Change and technology are intertwined, and any implementation requires strong project management.

First, say no to technology until you are ready to change your process. I have seen firms get excited and squander tens of thousands of dollars on the latest technology and either never use it or use it poorly. More often than not, that is because they tried to keep their existing way of doing things instead of first evaluating that process, making change, and then sourcing enabling technology.

Do not buy technology without the same level of work that you would put into a new car or house purchase, particularly with respect to your backbone system, like practice management. The costs of switching systems are high, even prohibitive.

However, lawyers do not easily relinquish control and want to do tasks that are better outsourced. Let's use marketing and optimizing your ranking or place on a Google search as an example. I went to both business and law school, and I know that you leave this to the experts. It makes no sense as an attorney to become a website or

Google expert. Instead, find someone and pay them to help you. That's just good business.

All that said, you must have some type of recordkeeping for your main workflow process. Think of a doctor's office without a system to keep appointments, send bills and keep your records – that is the same as not having a backbone or core system for your law firm.

Let's use Abe's new firm as an example of how to evaluate technology because, for the most part, the approach is the same regardless of practice area. Remember to keep in mind that there are two levels of costs to any implementation, even in a new firm. The real hard costs are the cash you spend on the software plus the cost of your time. The time that you devote to the new software selection, training and implementation is time that you are not doing client work, and that is a cost to keep in mind.

Evaluating Technology

Abe has mapped out how he is going to run his practice at a very high level. His next step is to find places where he can insert technology. There is a very long list of the types of technology you can use at a firm, but let's first outline about how you would choose technology.

- *Find technology that is simple to use.* Obviously, you are constrained by your budget, but you still need to look for simplicity because the number one reason that law firms don't adopt technology is that it is too much effort.

- *Ensure that you integrate the technology.* Part of sourcing simple software is to make sure that the new technology will work with your existing systems. You likely didn't open a firm to become a software guru, the chief information officer, or an IT professional, so systems need to easily work together.

- *Ask the software provider for case studies.* Reputable companies will have references and may have information on how their customers have measured the return on the money spent. Also, information on the type of users so that you don't buy a system that's really made for a much larger law firm.

- *Look outside of the law for solutions.* I know a solo lawyer who uses an accounting software as her practice management system. It captures the time by projects and she can load budgets to generate comparisons of budgeted versus actual amounts.

- *Ask for a trial or a free demo.* I believe that if somebody won't let you try the software in some way, you should find another vendor. You need to test for simplicity and how easy it is to learn. Also you need to imagine it working with your other software.

- *Ask for feedback from others.* Whether you ask your accountant for feedback on administrative software, a fellow attorney for their recommendations on legal solutions, or a trusted client to share their experience with a potential product, an outside perspective is critical.

- *Start small and build upon core systems.* Ensure all core systems are in the cloud and allow for information sharing. Also, essential functions like document signing, online billings and collections must be either part of the solution or easily added.

- *Free data migration.* For existing firms, this can be time-consuming so ensure that the software company will take care of it for you. Again, you are a lawyer; no need to become an IT professional.

If you are not opening a new practice, ensure that your technology, beyond a core system, is focused on where it can have the biggest impact or address your largest problem area.

Technology Plan: Solo Case Study

Abe has reviewed some articles on legal technology options and read product reviews. After chatting with fellow solos, he makes a list of all the possible technologies based on his new firm workflow plus a new category for software, which impacts the firm as a whole. He realizes that he must prioritize but also choose the core technology wisely to ensure that his software will work together simply. Also, given that Abe works alone, all his technology has to work equally well on a computer and a mobile device.

Workflow	Technology
Core	Scanning & Printing; Practice Management; Project Management; Mobile Device Management
Client Development (or marketing)	Virtual receptionist; Triage software; Online scheduling booking; client relationship management.
Client Intake (starting with engagement letter onwards)	Template Automation; Expert systems; E-signature; Chat-bot.
Legal Services Delivery (creation of work product, representation, all things practice of law)	Document Automation; Document Assembly; Research; Automated filing; Legal dictation; Document sharing & storage.
Billing and Collections (and financial reporting)	Accounting or bookkeeping; timekeeping; billing; online payment processing; collections.
Close & Measure Client Satisfaction (client feedback and also includes closing engagement)	Survey software; Template automation.

Abe is not starting with very many clients, so he decides to focus on the core technology plus some marketing software. With the startup and small business community, education is important because, like other legal matters, clients are often not sure what legal services they require.

Abe realizes that many of his clients are willing to access his site in the evening. However, he doesn't want them to just fill in a "contact us" form, but would rather have an interactive experience. He wants an inexpensive chat-bot that will answer some frequently asked questions and provide him with a snapshot of that chat. He will also have a quiz to gather information on the business needs with a link to a calendar that allows people to contact him for a quick free consult. He will also look for an expert system that can both triage further and educate the client. By also having a virtual receptionist service and voicemail that sends transcripts to his email, Abe will be accessible to all potential clients without actually being at the office.

Initially, Abe thought that he should hold off on purchasing a practice or project management system. However, one of his friends, an engineer, convinced him that if he set up his projects and his tasks from the start with a proper system, he would accumulate excellent data for pricing and time management. He will investigate small and inexpensive systems that can grow with his firm. Also, he will look at some of the free applications other attorneys use and make sure all are accessible on his phone and laptop.

Another good friend who works for a medium-sized law firm warned Abe that he should definitely research some of the mobile device management systems on the market to protect his client data. With all the security breaches, it is not unreasonable to protect his laptop and phone in the case of theft or loss.

Takeaways:

- Review and improve your processes before any technology purchase or new hire;

- Gather and analyze data before decisions; and

- Pay attention to cybersecurity issues regardless of firm size.

Conclusion

There is no end to change for either FFL or Abe. In other words, FFL will review other workflows and refine their focus on ideal clients. Abe's new firm will continue to experiment with new approaches and technology as it grows. The key to a healthy business is the ability to continuously adapt to change by relying on good data. In order to best lead your firm, meet with your team regularly to update firm goals, identify pain points and review processes.

Summary of Lessons Learned

Regardless of the data you collect, the changes you make to your firm, or the technology you choose to implement, these are common themes or lessons learned:

- **Design a Client-Centered Practice:** Your clients are the reason for your practice, so work on processes and offerings that best serve the client. Set and manage expectations and educate your client.

- **Be aware of your needs and challenges:** Data-driven decision making works best if you can identify your problems or areas in need of improvement to provide focus for your efforts. Your time to work on the administrative side of the firm is often limited, so be frugal with your resources and focus on the largest pain points.

- **Plan:** Set aside adequate time to create your overall plan of attack. Run it by a mastermind group or mentor. Do not try to change too much too fast.

- **Focus:** Part of your plan should be to set milestones and methodically focus on only one process or technology implementation at once. Remember that time is finite.

- **Delegate:** Unless you are a solo, routinely think of whether you are the best person within the firm for the task or project. Try to delegate as much as possible to train and grow your attorneys and staff, particularly if the task is non-legal.

- **Ask for help from outside your firm:** Change is not simple, so do not be afraid to reach out for help to understand your firm's challenges and to select or implement measures, new technology or processes.

- **Outsource:** You cannot do it all well, particularly if you are a solo. Find outside solutions and providers that are experts, for example, CPAs for your taxes, information technology experts for your network, hosting companies for the cloud and so on.

- **Buy Slow | Cancel Fast:** The same idea as hiring slow and firing fast. Take your time with your investment in change and technology, but if it's not working, stop spending the money and start over with a new approach.

One final word on always striving to improve and fostering a culture of change within your firm. Be open to change, but do not buy technology thinking that it will be the change catalyst. You need to resist technology until you settle upon a process. However, the solo and small law firm can use technology as an equalizer to offer legal services that compete with much larger firms on both price and quality. Finally, by using data and metrics you will be running your firm as a business and be on the road to success.

If you have any feedback or comments on this book, please reach out to me on twitter;

@maryjuetten

Appendix A: *All I Really Need to Know I Learned in Kindergarten* Quotes

These are the things I learned (in Kindergarten):

1. Share everything.

2. Play fair.

3. Don't hit people.

4. Put things back where you found them.

5. CLEAN UP YOUR OWN MESS.

6. Don't take things that aren't yours.

7. Say you're SORRY when you HURT somebody.

8. Wash your hands before you eat.

9. Flush.

10. Warm cookies and cold milk are good for you.

11. Live a balanced life - learn some and drink some and draw some and paint some and sing and dance and play and work every day some.

12. Take a nap every afternoon.

13. When you go out into the world, watch out for traffic, hold hands and stick together.

14. Be aware of wonder. Remember the little seed in the Styro-foam cup: The roots go down and the plant goes up and no-body really knows how or why, but we are all like that.

15. Goldfish and hamsters and white mice and even the little seed in the Styrofoam cup - they all die. So do we.

16. And then remember the Dick-and-Jane books and the first word you learned - the biggest word of all - "LOOK."

— Robert Fulghum, *All I Really Need to Know I Learned in Kindergarten*

Appendix B: Overall Approach

After collecting data, you can experiment with different ideas and trying to make your firm better for clients and you and your team. Below is the approach illustrated by the FFL example in the book. The most important takeaway from this chart is the green 'repeat' Post-it® note in the bottom right hand corner. Setting goals and analyzing pain points, bottlenecks, challenges or problems for all of your firm's processes should be *repeated* as you collect data and measure the impacts of your experiments and changes. And as we have demonstrated, you can do this without great expense using paper and markers. Embrace change as it's the only way forward for the legal profession.

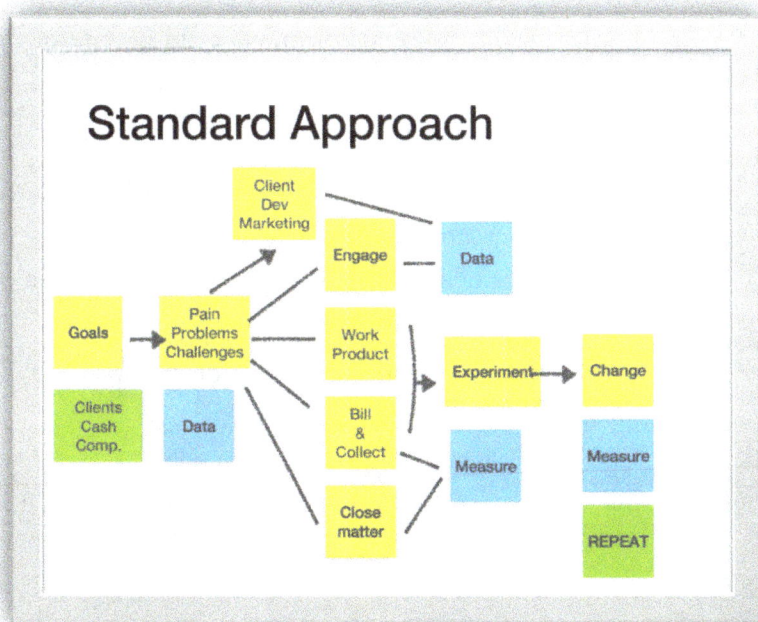

Appendix C: Technology Evaluation & Implementation Checklist

A final warning before you buy new technology. Always start by identifying and examining your problem areas. For example, there's no reason to buy software to enhance your billing process or collections if you are collecting everything within 30 days and you don't have a cash flow problem.

When choosing technology:

- Be open to change—review your process first;
- Find technology that is simple to learn and use;
- Less is more—start small and build upon each new product;
- Ensure that the data is moved from your old system for free;
- Check to make sure that the new system works easily with your existing core systems;
- Understand how to terminate the software agreement;
- Account for your costs beyond the cost of the software— your time at your billing rate for the project and add-on software licenses;
- Demand the following before making a decision:
  - o   user metrics;
  - o   case studies;
  - o   return on investment measured by clients;
  - o   client feedback; and
  - o   trial or free demo for you and client.

Bibliography

Ruth Carter, https://www.attorneyatwork.com/take-it-to-the-wall-organized/

Robert Fulghum, https://www.goodreads.com/book/show/34760.All_I_Really_Need_to_Know_I_Learned_in_Kindergarten 1986, Ballantine Books.

Mary Juetten, *Small Law Firm KPIs How to Measure your Way to Greater Profits.* 2016, Thomson Reuters available on Amazon: https://www.amazon.com/Small-Firm-Measure-Greater-Profits/dp/0314876014/.

Legal Trends Report Clio 2016 & 2017.

Scott Turow, *One L: The Turbulent True Story of a First Year at Harvard Law School. 2010, Farrar Straus Giroux.*

Benjamin H. Barton, *Glass Half Full: The Decline and Rebirth of the Legal Profession.* 2015, Oxford.